Praise for *Terror and Religion:*
An interfaith dialogue

When terrorists maim and murder, while proclaiming 'Allah is Great' – when Christians torture Christians for being the wrong sort of Christian – when the Torah recommends extermination of the Canaanite nations – who is to blame? Horrendous evils have been and are being committed in the name of the Abrahamic religions, so are we hiding from how hideous human nature can be?

When we blame religion for appalling atrocities are we passing the moral buck? After all, people plant the bombs; religious texts do not. In this fine trialogue, the participants grapple with the 'Who's to blame?' question: God, scriptural interpreters or humanity's innate nastiness? We meet the inconsistency of believers' talk of love and compassion while embracing religious recommendations for violence and destruction.

This is an excellent thought-provoking discussion; it takes us from scriptural incongruities of love and death urgings – to ways of passing the moral buck from God to humanity and back again – to wonderments at how religious jokes could ever justify murder of the jokers.

Does terrorism's blood drip from the scriptures, from God or from humanity and or even from *Charlie Hebdo*'s sense of humour or lack of sense? This book has no easy answers but is excellent at making us think – and reading and thinking are undoubtedly better than planting bombs, especially when we meet the odd joke or two.

Peter Cave,
Philosopher, Lecturer, Broadcaster, London, UK

With a lionhearted courage in facing this disputed topic, these three scholars, already familiar with each other's positions through two previous books, re-embark on a spirited interchange: they are honest, fearlessly critical of each other's perspective and daring in their enterprise. Their style is engaging – even occasionally humorous – and their integrity in dealing with their own faith and desire to be truthful is impressive. While agreeing on certain facts – each faith is culpable of terrible violence against humanity – they disagree in their conclusions. I welcome this book as an attempt to engage with one of our world's most terrifying threats.

Professor Mary Grey
Professor Emerita of Theology at the University of Wales

Abrahamic interfaith conversations amongst Jews, Christians and Muslims often suffer from the 'elephant in the room' effect, that is, the reluctance to address the Israeli–Palestinian conflict and other difficult issues. However, with the worrying rise in oppression, injustice and violence amongst the Abrahamic family across the world, there is no time like the present for far-ranging, candid and honest conversations. This trialogue from learned and experienced authorities and members of the Abrahamic faiths, covering a range of topics from sacred war and religious extremism to freedom of expression and end-days prophecies, is a much-needed inspiration for more fruitful global engagement amongst the religions.

Imam Dr Usama Hasan
Senior Researcher, Quilliam Foundation, UK

Exploring to what extent religion is part of the problem as well as the solution to violence and terror is the subject of this insightful dialogue between a Jewish, a Christian and a Muslim scholar. Each engages in an honest and impressively self-critical reflection on one of the most significant challenges of our time: religious radicalism and terror. Religious extremists turn to religious authority and scripture to justify their violence and hatred, and this book will help the reader understand the relationship between terrorism and religion.

Dr Ed Kessler MBE
Founder Director, Woolf Institute, Cambridge

The default position in history is the struggle for survival and therefore the use of violence. No wonder religion gets hauled in to add transcendent justification. The surprise, the miracle, is the appearance of groups which reject violence and territoriality, as found in Abrahamic and other faiths. The profound conversation in this book unravels the complexities of violence and its rejection in a manner very rarely achieved.

The Very Reverend Christopher Lewis
Emeritus Dean of Christ Church, Oxford

Terror and Religion
An interfaith dialogue

George D. Chryssides
Dan Cohn-Sherbok
Dawoud El-Alami

IMPRESS
BOOKS

First published 2016
by Impress Books Ltd
Innovation Centre, Rennes Drive,
University of Exeter Campus, Exeter EX4 4RN

Typeset in Palatino by Swales and Willis Ltd, Exeter, Devon

Printed and bound by Imprint Digital, UK

British Library Cataloguing in Publication Data

A catalogue record for this book is available from the British Library

ISBN: 978–1–907605–96–3 (pbk)
ISBN: 978–1–907605–97–0 (ebk)

To our respective wives Margaret, Lavinia and Kate, who have encouraged us throughout the project.

Contents

Foreword

Dialogue is one of the buzz words of our time. If we could only engage in dialogue, it is often assumed, peace would break out. But there is very little dialogue in the Socratic sense in the modern world; dialogue usually means trying to bludgeon your opponents into accepting your own position: it is not enough to seek the truth, we also have to humiliate and defeat our opponents. But Socrates, founder of the Western rational tradition, made it clear that dialogue required participants to subject every single one of their convictions to rigorous scrutiny. There was no point in entering a dialogue unless you were prepared to be changed and unsettled by the encounter and no one could 'win' a dialogue, because a Socratic dialogue as reported by Plato, always ends with the participants discovering that they knew nothing at all. And at that moment, Socrates said, they had become philosophers.

That is why this book is so important. It models exactly the kind of dialogue that is needed in our troubled times. It offers no solutions, but the three participants are listening to one another. We are good at talking these days, but not so good at listening. In a television debate, you can see that the participants are not really listening deeply to one another; they are simply thinking of the next brilliant remark that they are going to make. Here, the participants are listening to one another's pain and perplexity. They raise difficult questions for which there are no easy solutions.

They ask us: is religion inherently violent? We humans are violent creatures and our religious traditions reflect this. Indeed, historians of warfare tell us that civilization depends on the existence of well-regulated armies; they also insist that we never go to war for a single reason: there are always multiple interconnecting factors involved – territorial, political, cultural, social and economic. Experts on terrorism remind us that whatever its ideological stance, terrorism is always inherently political: it is about challenging the status quo or forcing a government to change a policy. Osama bin Laden was always very clear about his political goals. The leaders of ISIS may use (or abuse) religious rhetoric, but many of them were generals in Saddam's disbanded army – so they are secular, socialist Ba'athists. Making a scapegoat of 'religion' is too easy; it means that we are placing the blame elsewhere.

As for freedom of expression, Western people should remember that many of the political leaders who marched so righteously in Paris after the *Charlie Hebdo* atrocity had for decades supported regimes in Muslim-majority countries that had allowed their subjects no such *liberté*. The authors of this book remind us that everybody bears a measure of responsibility for the current plague of terrorism and that everybody has suffered. We need to emulate them by taking careful note of other people's pain. After the Paris shootings of 13 November 2015, the victims of the Beirut suicide bombing the previous day were forgotten. Perhaps we should have flown the Lebanese flag alongside the tricolour. In failing to do so, we in the West gave the impression that we regard some lives as more valuable than others.

If the reader finishes this book feeling confused and frustrated, has heard things that he or she did not want to hear, and is unable to see who – if anybody – is right, the authors will have accomplished something important. Only if we abandon our self-righteousness, learn that everybody bears a measure of responsibility for the horrors we experience today, and learn to empathise with other people's suffering do we have any hope of creating a peaceful, viable world.

Karen Armstrong, author of *Fields of Blood:
Religion and the History of Violence*

About the authors

George D. Chryssides studied Philosophy and Theology at the University of Glasgow, and gained his doctorate at the University of Oxford. He has taught at various British universities, becoming Head of Religious Studies at the University of Wolverhampton from 2001 to 2008. He is currently Visiting Research Fellow at York St John University. George has written extensively, focusing on new religious movements and on the Christian faith. Recent publications have included *Historical Dictionary of Jehovah's Witnesses* (2008), *Christianity Today* (2010), *Christians in the Twenty-First Century* (with Margaret Z. Wilkins, 2011), *Historical Dictionary of New Religious Movements* (2012), *The Bloomsbury Companion to New Religious Movements* (co-edited with Benjamin E. Zeller, 2014) and *Jehovah's Witnesses: Continuity and Change* (2016). He is a member of the Church of England and regularly attends Lichfield Cathedral.

Dan Cohn-Sherbok is an American rabbi and Professor Emeritus of Judaism at the University of Wales. He was educated at Williams College, Massachusetts, was ordained a Reform rabbi at the Hebrew Union College and received a Ph.D. from the University of Cambridge. Later he received an honorary D.D. from the Hebrew Union College-Jewish Institute of Religion, New York. He taught theology at the University of Kent where he was Director of the Centre for the Study of Religion and Society. He was subsequently Professor of Judaism at the University of Wales. He has written and edited over eighty books including *Judaism and Other Faiths* (1994), *Islam in a World of Diverse Faiths* (1991), *The Palestine–Israeli Conflict* (with Dawoud El-Alami, 2002), *Debating Palestine and Israel* (with Mary Grey, 2014) and *The Palestinian State: A Jewish Justification* (2012).

Dawoud El-Alami is of Palestinian heritage but was brought up in Egypt where he obtained the Licence en Droit from Cairo University and worked as a lawyer. He holds a Ph.D. from Glasgow University in Islamic Personal Status Law and has lived and worked in the UK for more than 30 years. He worked as a researcher at the Universities of Kent and Oxford and taught at Al al-Bayt University in Jordan in its inaugural year. He worked for 16 years at the University of Wales, Lampeter where he taught Islamic Studies and Islamic Law, and was course director of an M.A. in Religion and Politics. He and Dan Cohn-Sherbok taught parallel courses on the State of Israel and the Palestine Question. He is currently a Senior Lecturer at the University of Aberdeen. His specialist field is in Islamic Personal Status Law, but he has a strong interest in Middle Eastern history and politics.

Acknowledgements

A number of people have helped to make this book possible. Our spouses Margaret Wilkins, Lavinia Cohn-Sherbok and Kate El-Alami have offered support and encouragement throughout. Kate, additionally, has done much work on improving the text, and Margaret has performed the substantial task of compiling the index.

Thanks also are due to Richard Willis and the production staff at Impress Books, and also to Gay O'Casey, for her first-class copy editing. They have all been excellent to work with.

Introduction

On 7 January 2015 two masked gunmen forced their way into the *Charlie Hebdo* offices in Paris, armed with Kalashnikov rifles, which they trained on the journal's editorial staff, killing twelve. As they made their exit, they shouted 'Allahu Akbar!' ('God is great!'). They were also heard to say 'The Prophet is avenged'.

Despite *Charlie Hebdo*'s reputation for publishing outrageous cartoons that offended the sensibilities of many Muslims, the attack provoked an overwhelming response by the French population, many of whom took to the streets with placards bearing the slogan 'Je suis Charlie' ('I am Charlie'), demonstrating their solidarity with the journal, championing the cause of free expression and indicating that the freedom of the press would not be compromised by fear of terrorist attacks.

The event caused the three authors of this book – a Jew, a Christian and a Muslim – to write this dialogue, discussing the issues raised by the attack. Does free speech have its limits? Have we a right to object to seeing our faith blasphemed? Did the *Charlie Hebdo* cartoons amount to hate crimes? (One edition of the journal bore a front page cartoon depicting Muhammad saying '100 lashes if you don't laugh'; another had a caricature of Muhammad with a star covering his rectum, with the caption 'Mohammed: A star is born!') The editors pointed out that *Charlie Hebdo* was not specifically anti-Muslim, but also lampooned Jews and Christians. Does it make a difference if it is not merely a single faith that is targeted? And what about religious humour? Should a faith be strong enough to be unfazed by ridicule? Is it a different matter if a faith community tells jokes about themselves, rather than the jokes originating from those of another faith or no faith at all?

In the course of writing this book, further violent attacks and reactions to them occurred. ISIS (Islamic State of Iraq and Syria – also referred to as ISIL and Daesh) claimed responsibility for a bomb planted on a Russian plane on 31 October 2015, which exploded over Sinai, killing 224 passengers. Twelve days later, suicide bombers detonated explosives in Beirut, causing some forty persons to lose their lives. A day later the Paris attacks occurred: ISIS claimed responsibility for coordinated attacks on a concert hall, a stadium, and several bars and restaurants by suicide bombers and gunmen, who killed 130 and injured 368, many seriously. Our book entered its final stages of editing in April 2016, in the wake of reports of the attack on Brussels Airport and Metro, and further terrorist bombings in Aden, Baghdad and Lahore. Wikipedia provides a long list of terrorist attacks to which, if present trends continue, there may well be further additions that will have overtaken the events we have been able to mention.

The word 'Islamophobia' was current even before such acts of violence, describing an irrational fear of Muslims in general. Are all Muslims to be tarred with the same brush as the terrorists, or is Islam really a religion of peace, as its name etymologically implies? How typical are the so-called 'fundamentalists'? Republican US presidential candidate Donald Trump's desire to ban all Muslims from entering the country, and to require all Muslim US citizens to wear visible identification, indicates his perception that every Muslim poses a potential threat.

The ensuing discussion raises questions about attitudes to peace and to violence. All three religions see peace as their aim, yet none of them are inherently pacifist. So how do we reconcile peace and violence? In the following dialogue we look at some of the causes of violence. Terrorists do not engage in rifle attacks and suicide bombings simply because they have nothing better to do, so it is important to ask what motivates them. Is it religion itself? Some critics of religion, like Richard Dawkins, have contended that religion does more harm than good, and lies at the root of such evils. Others might point to perceived injustices, especially in connection with disputes about land that continue to occur in the Middle East, particularly Israel and its surrounding territory. Some have accused the media of sensationalising terrorism and fuelling bigotry and hatred.

Perhaps most importantly, what are the solutions? We consider the role of past crimes and resentments, and ask whether forgiveness and compromise might be possible. Followers of religions often claim that they are not understood aright, and we discuss ways of creating mutual understanding and bringing together people of different faiths. We do not claim to present miraculous solutions to the problems of violence that confront the world, but we hope that our discussion will at least help to identify the relevant issues, to locate the points our three faiths have in common and to highlight areas on which we cannot agree.

It should be clear to the reader that none of the three authors write as official spokespersons for their religions. The Jewish, Christian and Muslim faiths come in many different forms, and, of course, three different authors would no doubt have shed different perspectives on these matters. This is the third tripartite dialogue that we have published. *Why Can't They Get Along?* (Lion Books, 2014) spanned a range of controversial issues affecting our three faiths, and *Love, Sex and Marriage* (SCM Press, 2013) focussed on sexual morality and marital relationships. As with these previous dialogues, we have not sought to find common ground or to highlight points that members of our respective faiths would necessarily endorse. It is a frank but friendly exchange between exponents of the three Abrahamic faiths, and if our dialogue goes some way towards clarifying our respective beliefs and practices, and removing prejudices and misunderstandings, we will have achieved something of value.

CHAPTER 1

Teachings on violence

All three faiths have been associated with violence. What do our three faiths teach about violence? In this opening chapter, we outline our respective stances on violence and war in the light of our faiths' teachings.

Dan   During my second year at rabbinical seminary, all students in my class were required to register with the military chaplaincy. This was in preparation for graduation, when those of us who had not married would be required to enter one of the branches of the armed services. The Vietnam War was in progress, and there was a constant need for chaplains. Those who had families were exempt. I refused to go along with this scheme. I had no intention of serving in the army, and I also had deep reservations about the efficacy of armed conflict. To the astonishment of the seminary authorities, I declared that I wished to be registered as a conscientious objector.

I was summoned to the Dean's office for an interview. 'I am against war', I declared. 'Peace is all important. This is what the prophets taught. The Bible prophesies peace for all nations . . . The lion will lie down with the lamb, and all that.' For the next half hour my teachers pointed out that Judaism is not a pacifist religion. Indeed, the Hebrew Bible prescribes that war should take place against Israel's enemies.

Wars of extermination, for example, are referred to in several of Judaism's biblical commandments:

- Do not leave alive any individual of the seven Canaanite nations (Deuteronomy 20:16).

- Exterminate the seven Canaanite nations from the land of Israel (Deuteronomy 20:17).

- Always remember what Amalek did (Deuteronomy 25:17).

- The evil done to us by Amalek shall not be forgotten (Deuteronomy 25:19).

- Blot out the name (or memory) of Amalek (Deuteronomy 25:19).

The extent of such extermination is described in Deuteronomy 20:16–18 which orders the Israelites to 'not leave alive anything that breathes'.

In the history of ancient Israel, wars other than those of extermination often took place with Israel's enemies. Such conflicts were condoned on the grounds of self-defence. Nonetheless, there are strict rules about such warfare. Jewish law prohibits the use of outright vandalism. The 12th century rabbinic scholar Moses Maimonides wrote: 'On besieging a city in order to seize it, it must not be surrounded on all four sides but only on three sides, thus leaving a path of escape for whomever wishes to flee to save his life'. The Jewish philosopher Nachmanides, writing a century later, strengthened the rule and added a reason: 'We are to learn to deal kindly with our enemy'.

This is the background to modern warfare between Israel and its surrounding neighbours. In 1992, the Israel Defence Forces (IDF) drafted a Code of Conduct that combines international law, Israeli law, the Jewish heritage and the IDF's own traditional ethical code. Outside of Israel, there has also been concern about the rules for war in contemporary circumstances. In 2006 during the Lebanon War, for example, leaders of the Rabbinical Council of America issued a statement suggesting the Israeli military should review its policy of trying to spare the lives of innocent civilians, because Hezbollah puts Israeli men and women at risk by using their own civilians, hospitals, ambulances and mosques as human shields, cannon fodder and weapons of asymmetric warfare. Such discussion and debate is predicated on the assumption that armed struggle is justified when the lives of Jews are at stake.

George   I was born just at the end of the Second World War. My father registered as a conscientious objector, and probably gained exemption as a medical student. My mother was an out-and-out pacifist. Knowing my family's pacifist leanings, boys at school would ask me whether I thought that the British government should simply have allowed Hitler to dominate Europe, or – the perennial question for supporters of non-violence – what would I do if I were attacked by a potential killer? I had begun a strong commitment to the Christian faith, but I did not find clear answers, or even a clear position on war. 'Thou shalt not kill' was one of the Ten Commandments, but my church's minister – who was not a pacifist – explained that it was a prohibition on murder, not killing in general.

Certainly the ancient Israelites were no pacifists, although one might have argued that the ancient Israelites' bloody battles were superseded by the teachings of Jesus, the 'Prince of Peace'. Yet Jesus himself was capable of violence (although on a smaller scale) when he used a whip to drive the money-changers out of the Jerusalem Temple (John 2:15).

The Bible's teachings on war and violence are ambiguous. Its authors envision the final paradise as a state of lasting peace, where war, conflict and death will have ended: 'Nation will not take up sword against nation, nor will they train for war any more' (Isaiah 2:4). Yet Jesus says, 'Do not suppose that I have come to bring peace to the earth. I did not come to bring peace, but a sword' (Matthew 10:34). Before going out to the Garden of Gethsemane on the night of his arrest, he instructs his disciples to be armed: 'if you don't have a sword, sell your cloak and buy one' (Luke 22:36). When the disciples tell him that they have two swords among them, Jesus enigmatically replies, 'That's enough' (Luke 22:38). When his disciple Peter uses one of the swords to cut off the High Priest's servant's ear, Jesus commands him to put his sword away, adding, 'for all who draw the sword will die by the sword' (Matthew 26:51–52).

Throughout history, Christians have been involved in wars. The armed forces have their Christian chaplains, and at least one nuclear submarine has an Orthodox Christian chapel on board. Clergy are regularly involved in Remembrance Day celebrations, where the war dead are commemorated. On the other hand, the early Christians were victims rather than perpetrators of violence, and Church Fathers such as Clement of Alexandria, Tertullian and Origen opposed violence as a way of dealing with one's enemies. Christianity has given birth to several bodies committed to peace: the Mennonites, the Quakers, the Christian Campaign for Nuclear Disarmament (Christian CND), Pax Christi and many more, and Martin Luther King advocated non-violent methods for combating racial discrimination.

Most of us want to see a world of peace. But does this entail refusing to take up arms, or does challenging injustice sometimes involve armed conflict? Can war secure victory over evil, or does it simply determine which army is the more powerful? These are not easy questions, but in the dialogue that follows I hope we can at least explore some of the relevant issues.

Dawoud   I was born in Lebanon in 1953, just five years after my parents and eight siblings were displaced from their home and lands in Asqalan (Ashkalon) in Palestine where my brothers and sisters had been born. The loss was central to our family life and we knew who our enemies were and who had deprived us of our home.

From Lebanon we moved briefly to Jordan and then to Egypt where I was brought up in stability but always in the belief that one day the injustice would be righted and that we would go home.

The 1950s and 1960s were a time of secular nationalism throughout the region. We lived in a climate of war, which we felt was justified, but at that time there was no religious element to it. The founders of Arab nationalism had been both Muslim and Christian, including Michel Aflaq, a secular Christian who was perhaps the most important figure in Arab nationalism and the founder of the Arab Ba'ath Movement. Our parents and all those around us were morally behind the Arab cause, but my mother believed in building bridges, in solving problems by practical and peaceful means. She would not have been prepared to lose one of her children even for the return of all their lands.

At the time of the Six Day War I was 14 years old and the notion that our home was about to be liberated was exciting. We believed in the legitimacy of the armed struggle, so when the war ended in disaster and the loss of further territories in Sinai, the Golan, the West Bank and Jerusalem, we were devastated. I remember one of my teachers crying in the classroom because her husband had been taken prisoner by the Israelis. There was a sadness and humiliation that was not dispelled until the October War in 1973. At no time, however, did we examine the issues in religious terms – it was purely a case of right and wrong. Although religion was a part of daily life and all around us in an organic way, it did not really become part of the dialogue around the conflict and the politics of the region until the 1970s when there was the beginning of an Islamic resurgence as a reaction to dictatorship and injustice. In Egypt in particular it was a reaction to the perception that while the economy was growing and being opened up to international markets, it was still only the privileged classes who were benefitting from economic development while the masses struggled. This allowed the Muslim Brotherhood, which had been incubating quietly for decades, to re-emerge as a powerful force based on its original principles of social justice. The notion of jihad or holy war had until this point not arisen as a central concept in the context of the Palestinian struggle and the adoption of the Palestinian cause by the Egyptians who had sacrificed so much.

Dan   I have always been troubled by the tension George refers to between peace and violence in the Christian tradition. From New Testament times to the present, Christian preachers have focused on Jesus' compassion and mercy. Yet the Church itself has embraced violence in spreading its message. Some years ago I wrote a book entitled *The Crucified Jew: Twenty Centuries of Christian Antisemitism* (1997). Its thesis was that we Jews have been persecuted and murdered by Christians for nearly two millennia. During the Middle Ages, for example, Jewish communities throughout Europe were destroyed by Christian fanatics. Under the Inquisition, Jews were tortured and burned at the stake for their beliefs. Here is what Luther had to say about the Jews in *On the Jews and Their Lies*:

> First, their synagogues should be set on fire, and whatever does not burn up should be covered or spread over with dirt so that no one may ever be able to see a cinder or stone of it . . . Secondly, their homes should likewise be broken down and destroyed. (Cohn-Sherbok, 1992:73)

More recently, the Holocaust crystallised previous centuries of Christian antipathy towards Jewry. Six million Jews were slaughtered in an attempt to rid Western civilisation of a Jewish presence. Although such an onslaught was fuelled by a racist rather than religious ideology,

Nazi crimes were often perpetrated by believing Christians. Although a number of Christian leaders sought to defend Jews from attack, many Christians simply refused to be drawn into this conflict, including those in positions of ecclesiastical influence. For example, when asked by the Vichy government in France about the antisemitic law promulgated in France on 2 June 1941, the Vatican declared: 'In principle, there is nothing in these measures which the Holy See would find to criticise' (Cohn-Sherbok, 1992: 209). Is it any wonder that many Jews are suspicious of Christians and Christianity and fearful of missionary activities?

Turning to Dawoud's reflections about the Palestinian–Israeli conflict, he is right that Israel is engaged in an armed struggle against Palestinians. It is a tragedy that it has not proved possible for Jews and Arabs to live together in peace. When the Balfour Declaration was issued in 1917, the British had hoped that the indigenous Arab population in Palestine would be able to live harmoniously with their Jewish neighbours. But, the Palestinians viewed Jews in their midst as usurpers. From the earliest stages of Jewish immigration, Palestinians sought to overturn the Balfour Declaration, and in a series of devastating attacks and wars, they have sought to drive Jews into the sea.

Recently we have witnessed the emergence of violent jihad promoted by Muslims who seek to wage a holy war against the West. Originally the concept of 'jihad' referred to a spiritual internal struggle, but in the minds of a significant number of believers it has been understood in military terms. Such an armed campaign has to be declared by a proper authority and advised by scholars who say that the Muslim faith and people are under threat and the use of violence is imperative to defend them. Some Muslim scholars argue against this interpretation and insist that jihad should not be understood as a declaration of war against the enemies of Islam. Here – as in Christianity – there is a serious, unresolved tension between peace and violence.

George The Christian position on war is complex, and not unanimous. The early Christians did not engage in armed combat. They could not afford to as, being a small religious minority, they were not capable of physical opposition to the Roman authorities. Instead they offered non-violent resistance and, where necessary, underwent martyrdom. The alternative was apostasy.

Once Christianity became allied to Roman power, things changed. The Emperor Constantine purportedly had a vision of a cross in the sky, and heard a voice saying, 'In this sign conquer!' Being a Christian subsequently became compatible with being a soldier – a notion that Augustine of Hippo (354–430) endorsed when he wrote that God's servants could legitimately use swords (Romans 13:4). However, Augustine did not advocate indiscriminate violence: where there was a grave wrong to be put right, one had a duty to use force against the perpetrator.

Augustine's views on war marked the beginning of the Church's doctrine of the just war, particularly associated with Roman Catholic teaching. A number of criteria had to be satisfied for war to be legitimate. First and foremost, the cause had to be just: expansionist military policies could no longer be condoned. Second, there had to be a probability of success: to experience the casualties of war without having furthered one's cause is to be in a worse situation than before. Third, war must be authorised by proper civil authorities, rather than private armies or terrorist organisations. Fourth, the benefits of victory must outweigh the losses that are incurred through armed combat. Finally, war must be a last resort: since no one wants to sustain the death and injury incurred in war, it is only humane to consider whether one's aims might be attained through negotiation, or whether it is better to endure the status quo.

Modern developments in weaponry, especially the proliferation of nuclear weapons, have caused some Christians to consider whether any benefits of winning a large-scale war could possibly justify the losses incurred – hence the rise of organisations like Christian CND. Other Christians, however, particularly in the evangelical Protestant tradition, see 'wars and rumours of wars' as signs of the last days (Mark 13:7), and an inevitable prelude to the coming battle of Armageddon. Since the name Armageddon may refer to the Plain of Megiddo, these Christians have viewed affairs in the Middle East as signs of the coming apocalypse and fulfilments of biblical prophecy.

Whether or not Jews, Christians and Muslims are acting out a pre-determined divine plan, Dan is right in locating causes of conflict in the past and not simply the present. The Christian history of antisemitism continues to fuel conflicts between Christians and Jews, and Dawoud is charitable not to mention the ways in which Christians have attacked Muslims, for example in the Crusades. (Of course the Christians have not always been the perpetrators of violence.) In the discussion that follows, we have all agreed to be forthright about our views, but we also need to consider how we come to terms with our past and move forward. The Christian faith does not require complete non-violence, yet Christians hope for lasting peace. How our three faiths can achieve this in the light of our past is a formidable challenge.

Dawoud   It is not strictly true to say, as Dan has suggested, that jihad was originally a concept of spiritual struggle, although many scholars have interpreted it to include this meaning. It is in its origins, unequivocally, a call to fight in the way of God. The injunctions to jihad are not, however, a call to offensive war but to the defence of Islam and Muslims against hostile enemies. Wars have played a prominent role in the history of Islam from its origins in the Arabian Peninsula in the 7th century, but this does not mean that Islam is essentially a warlike religion. The early message of Islam was not a call to arms, but a call to faith in the one God and the rejection of idolatry.

The early Muslims faced violent opposition, however, from Quraysh, the dominant tribe which controlled the Ka'aba and the polytheistic cult, which was inextricably linked to its role as a centre of trade and pilgrimage, and whose vested interests were therefore threatened by the rejection of its gods. Inter-tribal raiding had been part of the way of life and the economy of the tribes of the Arabian Peninsula, but following the success of the Muslims in gaining control of Mecca, the Prophet Muhammad formed alliances and treaties with tribes throughout the peninsula cemented by religious unity and personal loyalty. The Hadith comprises a number of rules of warfare established by the Prophet, including the instruction that conflict should not be sought but only entered into where this is unavoidable; women, children, the sick and elderly, monks and people in places of religious worship should not be killed; towns and houses should not be burnt; there should be no treachery or mutilation; trees and crops should not be destroyed and animals should not be slaughtered except as necessary for food.

Through a combination of conflict, diplomacy and trade, Islam came to dominate the peninsula and began to expand into neighbouring regions. In Syria, the Persian and Byzantine Empires were exhausted by two centuries of religious war against each other, and the coming of Islam brought peace, stability and prosperity to the region. In the areas that the Muslim rulers came to dominate, they largely insisted that the Arab armies be garrisoned away from cities and towns to avoid disruption of society and the economy. They did not seek to plunder and destroy existing centres of civilisation, but to control, maintain and develop them. They established systems under which Muslims, Christians and Jews could co-exist peacefully while retaining their own religious identity.

Throughout the history of Islam there have been long periods when communities of the three monotheistic faiths have lived together in security and prosperity, but there have also been times of bitter conflict. From the Crusades to the dismantling of the Ottoman Empire and the carving up of the Arab World, the displacement of the Palestinians by the creation of Israel and the conflicts since the first invasion of Iraq in 1990–1991, the source of conflict has often come from external interference.

The longest standing and most bloody conflict is not, however, that of Islam with other religions, but that within the body of Islam itself, between the Sunna and the Shi'a. This has its origins in the dispute over the succession to the Prophet, and the bloodshed of the 7th century is still felt amongst these communities as if it were yesterday. It remains at the heart of the conflicts of the Middle East even today.

CHAPTER 2

Misunderstandings

Each of us agrees that there are ways in which our faiths are commonly misunderstood. We discuss common misunderstandings which are relevant to the issues of terror, war and violence, and consider how exclusivist versions of our faiths can foster misconceptions, and result in violent expressions of the three faiths.

George Hostility often comes through misunderstandings of one another's faith, and misunderstandings of Christianity abound – not only among Jews and Muslims, but unfortunately among Christians themselves. In our previous book *Why Can't They Get Along?* (2014) we explored a number of misconceptions: that the doctrine of the Trinity entails that Christians worship three gods; that the Gospels – particularly St John – are antisemitic; that Jesus claimed to supersede Moses, and so on.

Perhaps more worrying are misunderstandings among Christians themselves. Especially in the evangelical Protestant tradition, in which I was reared, the only true Christians were regarded as those who had undergone a conversion experience in which they had 'asked the Lord Jesus into their hearts', accepted the Gospel on faith, believed the Bible to be the inerrant word of God, and Jesus Christ as the sole means of salvation. The Bible, some evangelical preachers claimed, was God's 'instruction manual', which offered all the solutions to all life's problems. When confronted with a difficult situation, one only needed to think of Jesus, and ask what he would have done – an idea that is now propagated in the popular 'What Would Jesus Do' (WWJD) movement. Jesus taught that love was the greatest commandment in the Jewish Law, so – these people say – loving one's neighbour, and also one's enemy, is the cure for the world's problems.

I once heard a Christian in this tradition say that he had travelled to Glasgow but was disappointed to find only half a dozen real Christians there! This was hardly surprising if he was looking for those who held the same narrow view of the Christian faith as himself. What he failed to recognise was that his version of Christianity was only one of a large spectrum of Christian positions. There are an estimated 44,000 Christian denominations worldwide, with some 350 affiliated to the World Council of Churches. These include evangelical and liberal Protestants, Roman Catholics, Eastern Orthodox, Pentecostals, Anglicans and Lutherans. Some believe in the infallibility of scripture, while others regard the Bible as inspired but a book which must be subjected to critical examination. Its key characters often fall far short of perfection, but illustrate the struggle to bring about God's kingdom of peace and justice.

Some Christians remain exclusivist. Jesus said, 'No one comes to the Father except through me' (John 14:6), and these words have prompted the missionary quest to win the world for Christ. I doubt if Jesus was asserting the supremacy of Christianity. The eve of his death, when defeat by the religious and political authorities was imminent, was hardly the moment for a rallying call to replace other world faiths with Christianity, which had not even emerged as a separate religion.

Half a century ago, Pope Paul VI wrote about other faiths his encyclical *Nostra Aetate* ('In Our Time'): 'The Catholic Church rejects nothing that is true and holy in these religions. She regards with sincere reverence those ways of conduct and of life.' Christians therefore hold different views on exclusivism, other faiths, war and violence. Their views and actions have sometimes been harsh and offensive, but in the discussion that follows I hope that Dan and Dawoud will allow that Christians change, and that the views of any one particular exponent of the faith are not necessarily my own.

Dawoud George has identified a very important point, which is that misunderstandings and differences of doctrine and practice within a faith can sometimes be more difficult to reconcile than differences with other religions. Like Christianity, Islam has numerous branches and denominations but, as mentioned in the previous chapter, the main division is that between the Shi'a and the Sunna which dates back almost fourteen centuries. Sunni Muslims consider themselves to be the orthodox majority and wholly reject the claims of the Shi'a to the direct succession to the Prophet in the line of his daughter Fatima and her husband Ali ibn Abi Talib, his cousin. As the fourth of the Rightly Guided Caliphs, Ali and his descendants through Fatima are respected and even revered by both Sunna and Shi'a as the only descendants of the Prophet.

The character of Ali as the first male convert, a pious Muslim and just ruler is admitted by all denominations. Ali's son Al-Husayn was martyred at the battle of Karbala in Iraq and this event is commemorated annually on the Day of Ashura, which is a day of mourning at which profound grief is expressed through various rituals including, in some places, self-flagellation by male mourners. For Shi'i Muslims the division is seen as a conflict between the justice and piety of Ali and the corruption of his adversaries. There are further denominations within the Shi'a including the Ithna'ashriya (also known as Imami or Ja'fari Shi'a) Zaidis and Isma'ilis, and various subdivisions of each. Within Sunni Islam a number of ideological and political movements have arisen since the 18th century, including Wahhabism, Salafism and the Muslim Brotherhood, as well as various offshoots of these. Nothing compares, however, to the bitter legacy of this first rift which tore the early Muslim community apart violently and forever.

I think there is a failure amongst non-Muslims, including those involved in the political affairs of the Islamic world, to understand this. We hear the terms Sunni and Shi'ite on the news, but for most people this means very little. In the 1980s following the Iranian Revolution, the term Shi'a was almost synonymous with extremist or even terrorist attitudes, while today the Shi'a are more often viewed as the oppressed victims of Sunni regimes, although understanding of the background to this is limited. I do not think that this is restricted to the understanding of Islam, however. It is also probably true that it is too easy for each of our faiths to see the others as monolithic and this can be the cause of misunderstanding. Muslims, for example, very often do not recognise the distinction between Jews in their many religious and secular denominations throughout the world and Israelis. Most have only limited if any understanding of the distinction between Christian denominations.

George refers to the exclusivist beliefs of some Christians. For Muslims there is an absolutism in the belief that Islam is God's final revelation and the culmination and completion of the earlier revealed religions, Judaism and Christianity. They are, however, enjoined to respect and protect the 'people of the book', namely Christians and Jews living amongst them.

Dan   There are grave misunderstandings about Judaism as well. Most textbooks which outline Jewish history, belief and practice give the impression that the Jewish faith is monolithic in character. But this has not been true in the past. And it is certainly not the case in the present. In Hellenistic times, for example, there were three major groups: Sadducees, Pharisees and Essenes who interpreted the Jewish heritage in very different ways. Later in the early medieval period the Karaites rejected rabbinic Judaism. In the 17th century the Shabbateans believed that Shabbetai Tzevi was the long-awaited Messiah and broke with the rabbinic establishment. In more recent times the Hasidim embraced kabbalistic doctrine and sought to infuse Judaism with mystical fervour.

Modern Judaism has witnessed an even more profound division of the Jewish world. On the far right, strictly Orthodox Jews including the Hasidim believe that every word in the Pentateuch (Genesis, Exodus, Leviticus, Numbers and Deuteronomy) was given by God to Moses on Mount Sinai. This means that all 613 commandments recorded in Scripture must be obeyed (along with the rabbinic interpretation of these laws). Moving along the religious spectrum, Conservative Judaism has broken with tradition and stresses the need to modernise the Jewish heritage. Adopting a more radical approach, Reform Judaism considers as relevant only those Jewish laws which are spiritually meaningful in contemporary society. Both Reconstructionist and Humanistic Judaism are non-theistic in character, rejecting a belief in a supernatural deity who intervenes in human history. So you can see that it is a mistake to think that Judaism is uniform in nature. There is truth in the Jewish joke that when you have three Jews, you have six different opinions!

You might be surprised to learn that Jews cannot even agree about who is Jewish. Up until the last century, it was universally accepted that anyone born of Jewish maternal descent is a Jew. Alternatively, if a person is converted by an Orthodox bet din (Jewish court), that individual is Jewish. However, Orthodox Jews reject converts who have been converted by other denominations. To make matters more confusing, the Reform movement in the United States in the 1980s decreed that children of Jewish paternal descent (who were previously regarded as non-Jews) are in fact Jewish as long as they have participated in Jewish life by attending religious school, having a bar mitzvah or undergoing confirmation. The situation has become even more bewildering following the decision of the State of Israel to recognise certain individuals as Jewish and permit them to settle in Israel even though Orthodox authorities do not regard them as Jews.

Concerning Israel itself, it is a mistake to think – as many do – that all Jews are Zionists and support Israel's policies. Anti-Zionists in Arab lands as well as critics of Israel in other countries frequently make this error and criticise Jewry in general for Israel's policies regarding the Palestinians, but in fact in Israel itself the population is deeply divided, with political parties ranging from extreme Zionists on the far right to bitter critics of the government on the left. In the diaspora there are many Jews who are highly critical of the current state of affairs and seek peace and reconciliation with the Palestinians. A sizeable number favour the creation of a Palestinian state and a just solution to the Palestinian–Israeli conflict. For them, and I count myself in this number, violence and war are no way forward.

George   Exclusivism can certainly be an important contributor to violence, causing those making exclusive claims to truth to coerce others into accepting them. No doubt this has been done with the intention of saving people's souls, but the cost has been the hunting of heretics and the burning of witches. Jews and Muslims, as well as Christians, have committed acts of violence in the name of establishing true religion. The Hebrew scriptures contain many accounts of Yahweh's idol-rejecting followers seeking to expunge Canaanite fertility worship, even to the extent of committing acts of genocide. In Iran the Baha'i – a peace-loving religious community – have suffered cruel persecution, their sole offence being that they acknowledge their founder-leader Baha'u'llah as the prophet of the present era, thus denying that Muhammad is the culmination of the line of God's prophets.

However, it would be a gross misunderstanding to suppose that all followers of all three faiths are exclusivist. Jesus said that the way that leads to eternal life is a narrow one, and that it is a wide gate that leads to destruction (Matthew 7:13–14). Some have taken this to mean that it is only through the Christian faith that salvation can be gained, but this is not what Jesus said: he was merely pointing to the stringent demands of following his teachings. Christians who are more liberal have sometimes pointed to Jesus' statement, 'My father's house has many rooms' (John 14:2), regarding it as a hint that God's kingdom will contain others who have followed different spiritual paths. The notion of a god who would subject non-believers either to eternal punishment or to oblivion makes him morally worse than the world's greatest tyrant. Exterminating every non-believer would be genocide on a much larger scale than perpetrated by Adolf Hitler, Pol Pot, Saddam Hussein, the Rwandan Hutus and many more, all combined!

The idea of a vengeful God, as is sometimes found in Hebrew scriptures, has caused some Christians to claim that the God of the Old Testament is a God of wrath, while the God of the New Testament is a God of love. But this too is a misunderstanding. The Christians consciously appropriated the scriptures of the Jews, and are faced with the task, in common with Jewish believers, of making sense of them. The Hebrew scriptures also portray God as a god of love: Jeremiah, for example, writes, 'I have loved you with an everlasting love' (Jeremiah 31:3), and the Psalms are full of references to God's love for his people.

The Bible is best understood as a record of how God dealt with his people in the course of their history, and the events it recounts are not always to their credit. The Jews gained their land by destroying the resident Canaanites, and by subsequent expansionist military policies that reached their zenith with King David. King Solomon commissioned the building of the Jerusalem Temple, but at the price of enforced labour and high taxation. The Jews' acquisition of their territory has therefore historically been by morally questionable means, despite the fact that many Jews – supported by Christian Zionists – regard the land as theirs, and any claim that they are the rightful divinely approved inheritors as a consequence of their history must be subjected at best to critical scrutiny.

Dawoud   I think in the case of all our faiths and their various denominations, many of the problems of misunderstanding arise out of the popular understanding of the religions and their teachings, and not out of their core meanings. For Muslims, all three of the Abrahamic faiths have the same origin. Islam recognises Abraham as the father of all three communities and acknowledges many of the biblical prophets, including Moses and Jesus, as prophets of Islam. Muslims consider Abraham to have been the first Muslim in the sense of a person who surrenders to the One God. They consider that it was he and his son Ismail who built the Ka'aba in Mecca as the house of God. God sent messengers and divine scriptures to previous generations, culminating in the Prophet Muhammad, the Seal of the Prophets who brought the Qur'an, the final and infallible message to humankind.

The Qur'an contains versions, sometimes with variations of detail or emphasis, of many Biblical narratives delivered in a shorthand form that appears to assume existing knowledge of the stories of the Prophets and their messages. It mentions specifically the *Zabur* or Psalms of David, the *Tawrat* or Torah of Moses and the *Injil* or Gospel of Jesus and it refers to Jews and Christians as 'People of the Book', making it clear that they are part of the same tradition. Nowhere are Jews and Christians excluded from reward in the hereafter. According to the biography of the Prophet, at the start of his mission to deliver the message of monotheism, the first person he consulted other than his wife was her cousin Waraqa, a Christian, who confirmed the validity of the message. Some 7 years before the Hijra, the emigration from Mecca to Madina, according to the Sira literature (the biography of the Prophet and early history of Islam), a group of early Muslims fled persecution in Mecca and sought refuge with the *Najashi* or Negus in *Habash* (Abyssinia), thought to refer to the Christian King of Aksum who was known to be a just and pious ruler. Accounts in early Islamic literature relate how the ruler listened to the Muslims describing their faith and, asserting that there was no meaningful difference between them, granted them asylum.

From the outset then, Islam was inclusive of the other monotheistic traditions, but there is an absolutism in the fundamental tenet that the Qur'an is the final revelation to humankind, the literal and infallible word of God, and that Muhammad is God's last messenger. This has been combined with the belief, supported by the Qur'an, that Christians and Jews altered and corrupted their scriptures, and that this is the reason for the contradictions that exist between the Qur'an and the Bible.

This has led to an underlying exclusivism which has permeated Islamic popular culture and belief. It is this exclusivism and absolutism that allows zealots and those with political agendas to seek and select textual evidence for all manner of atrocities and breaches of the fundamental rights and freedoms of others. It is, however, equally possible to find a Qur'anic basis for peaceful coexistence and mutual respect and regard between the religions.

Dan We have been discussing various misunderstandings and misrepresentations of our faiths, and I want to focus on a key religious issue that has profound political implications today. In my earlier exchange in this chapter, I emphasised that strictly Orthodox Jews regard the Five Books of Moses (the Pentateuch) as divinely revealed. This doctrine is referred to in Hebrew as Torah Mi Sinai (Torah from Sinai). Based on the Hebrew Bible, many Orthodox religious Zionists in Israel and the diaspora maintain that Eretz Israel (the land of Israel) was promised by God to the ancient Israelites. Consequently they believe that Jews have a permanent and inalienable right to the land. Central to this vision is the conviction that Jerusalem is a symbol of the Holy Land and their return to it is promised by God in numerous biblical prophecies.

Such groups as Gush Emunim (Bloc of the Faithful) contend that Zionism is not simply a political movement; rather, it was used by God to initiate the return of the Jews to the land promised to Abraham, Isaac and Jacob. It is God's will that the Jewish people return to their home to establish a Jewish sovereign state in which they can live according to the laws of Torah and halakhah. In their view, it is a mitzvah (good deed) to cultivate the land. Therefore, settling in Israel is an obligation on religious Jews everywhere.

A sizeable number of Orthodox Jews throughout the world focus on this one central theme in Scripture: God's promise of the land to Abraham, Isaac and Jacob. As a consequence they believe that the Holy Land belongs to the Jewish nation. This is a divine mandate and a crucial element in God's providential plan for his chosen people. It would be a mistake, however, to assume that all Jews subscribe to this theology. Amongst a number of Jews who reject biblical fundamentalism but look to Scripture for guidance and spiritual inspiration, there is a different perspective. Influenced by themes of liberation and freedom in Scripture and the rabbinic tradition, they stress that God is on the side of the poor and the oppressed. The Book of Exodus, they point out, declares that God heard the groaning of the ancient Israelites and remembered the covenant with them. God took sides with his chosen people, stating that they would be liberated from their oppressors.

From this act of deliverance, Jews have constantly derived a message of hope. If God was on the side of the oppressed in ancient times, surely he will continue to take sides with the downtrodden of all ages. In the view of these Jewish liberationists, Jews today must view the Middle East conflict in moral terms. In the contemporary world where Jews are often comfortable and affluent, the prophetic message of liberation can easily be forgotten. Yet, a Jewish theology of liberation – with its focus on the desperate situation of those at the bottom of society – can act as a clarion call, awakening the people of Israel to their divinely appointed task.

Now that the Jewish nation has re-established itself in Eretz Israel after centuries of exile, these Jewish activists stress that what is now needed is for Jews worldwide to turn their attention to the Palestinian problem. The Jewish longing for statehood has been fulfilled. As an empowered people, Jewry should now empower those who cry out in their distress. In their view, God's promise to Abraham, Isaac and Jacob must not be allowed to overshadow the Bible's commitment to the liberation of all God's people.

CHAPTER 3

Peace as an ideal

None of our three faiths is inherently pacifist, and they believe that war and violence can at times be justified. Yet all three religions see peace as the ultimate goal to be achieved. How do we resolve this paradox? Is it possible to aim at peace, yet justify war?

Dawoud   The message of the Qur'an is quite clear – that every human life is precious and the taking of life is forbidden except as lawful penalty for murder and the worst of crimes:

> We decreed upon the Children of Israel that whoever kills a soul unless for a soul or for corruption in the land – it is as if he had slain mankind entirely, and whoever saves one – it is as if he had saved mankind entirely. (5:32)

There are, however, in a number of verses, injunctions to fight in the way of God, in self-defence or defence of one's family, to preserve the faith and to protect and defend Muslims and oppressed and displaced peoples.

Those who have been attacked are permitted to take up arms because they have been wronged – God has the power to help them – [they are] those who have been driven unjustly from their homes only for saying, 'Our Lord is God. If God did not repel some people by means of others, many monasteries, churches, synagogues and mosques, where God's name is much invoked, would have been destroyed. God is sure to help those who help his cause – God is strong and mighty' (22:39–40).

Fighting should only be for justifiable reasons, and should not go beyond what is strictly necessary to restore order, justice and security for the people – it should be strictly proportional:

> Fight in God's cause against those who fight you, but do not overstep the limits: God does not love those who overstep the limits. Kill them wherever you encounter them, and drive them out from where they drove you out, for persecution is more serious than killing. Do not fight them at the Sacred Mosque unless they fight you there. If they do fight you, kill them – this is what such disbelievers deserve – but if they stop, then God is most forgiving and merciful. Fight them until there is no more persecution, and [your] worship is devoted to God. If they cease hostilities, there can be no [further] hostility, except towards aggressors. (2:190–194)

Some scholars have pointed out that while the just war theory only developed in Christianity during the 4th century as Christianity was not involved in government and statecraft before that period, its development in Islam was catalysed at the outset by the emergence of Islam not only as a religion but also at the same time as a political entity requiring practical policies and government.

One of the branches of the science of Qur'anic exegesis is Asbab al-Nuzul or the reasons for revelation. This examines the text in the context of the events of the period of the revelation. It is believed that certain verses were revealed specifically in relation to events at the time, often addressed directly to the Prophet and his followers. Some verses appear to condone aggressive action against non-believers, but they may be interpreted to refer to the specific context of the struggle of the early Muslim community against its oppressors.

George   Theologically, the Christian faith teaches that the ultimate cause of war and violence is sin. While peace is the ideal, a sinful world falls short of the standard that God requires, and until a perfect society is achieved, there will be human conflicts.

The mention of sin possibly makes me sound like the Bible-brandishing street preacher in the town centre and whose rant causes passers-by to hurry past in embarrassment. The problem with most street preachers is that they don't offer practical solutions to specific issues involving sin. To ask people to repent is to leave them without any guidance as to whether they should abandon violence or engage in armed conflict in a just war.

The word 'sin', of course, is meant to make people feel uncomfortable, and the Christian doctrine of sin is that it proliferates. The doctrine of 'original sin' – particularly emphasised by Protestants – entails that Adam's sin affected the entire human race, and more radical reformers like John Calvin championed the doctrine of humanity's 'total depravity'. If this seems an unduly pessimistic view of human nature, it is an interesting exercise to reflect on how many of the news headlines each day are about human wrong-doing.

War is part of humanity's sinful condition, and it can also proliferate, since an unjust outcome in armed conflict is a cue for further hostilities. The problem about the doctrine of the just war, to which I referred earlier, is not only about identifying when a cause is a just one. Unfortunately, wars do not ensure that justice is achieved, but merely determine which of the opposing parties is stronger. It is not like going to a court of law, where – at least most of the time – one can expect a just outcome. Where might rather than right prevails, the seeds are sown for further combat, as happened with the Second World War, which was at least in part prompted by the 1919 Treaty of Versailles, ending the previous major conflict but thought to be unjust by the Germans.

If only we could break the chain of hostility! Some Christians have taken the view that the solution to armed conflict is non-participation: 'There would be no wars if we refused to fight'. This stance has been taken by the Quakers, who have only accepted non-combative wartime roles, and leaders like Martin Luther King who advocated non-violent activism to conquer injustice.

The Bible often uses military imagery in portraying the fight against sin. Paul (or someone writing with his name) talks about the armour of God, and fighting the good fight of the faith (Ephesians 6:13; 1 Timothy 6:12). Such imagery may appear to condone the use of physical force where it is needed, although with the kinds of constraint that Dawoud mentions. However, the Christian faith teaches the need for something more powerful than physical weapons. Paul writes, 'The weapons we fight with are not the weapons of the world. On the contrary, they have divine power to demolish strongholds' (2 Corinthians 10:4).

Perhaps the street-preacher has a point, however badly he expresses it. Sin requires repentance – a radical transformation of ourselves. As St Ambrose (c.334–397) said, 'The greatest danger does not lie outside us. It comes from our very selves: the enemy is within'.

Dan I think you need to keep in mind that the Jewish people have been in existence for nearly four millennia. Judaism is thus a far older religion than Christianity and Islam. From the beginning the Hebrews were a minority group living in a hostile environment. According to the Torah, they were persecuted and enslaved in Egypt. Scripture teaches that God delivered them from bondage and led them to the Promised Land. At Passover we celebrate this act of deliverance. And we are reminded of the numerous occasions in our history when enemies have assailed us. The Passover Haggadah relates the divine pledge that despite our tribulations, God will be with us:

> It is this Divine pledge that has stood by our fathers and by us also. Not only one man hath risen against us to destroy us, but in every generation men have risen against us to destroy us: but the Holy One delivereth us always from their hand.

When the Jewish nation was established in Israel in ancient times, Jews armed themselves in defence. However, following the Babylonian captivity in the 6th century BCE, the Southern Kingdom (Judah) was dominated by foreign powers for hundreds of years. Eventually, in the first century Jews sought to overthrow Roman rule but were defeated. From that time until the 20th century Jews have lived as a minority people in foreign lands. In these circumstances, they were unable to defend themselves from attack. Instead, Jewry longed for the arrival of a divinely appointed Messiah who would deliver them from exile. This messianic hope sustained Jews who repeatedly experienced contempt and hostility. This vision was one of peace as predicted by the biblical prophets and expounded by rabbinic sages – with the coming of the Messiah, peace will reign throughout the world and war and violence will cease. This has been the hope of the Jewish people throughout their turbulent history, a longing for harmony among all the nations.

Yet, the Messiah has not come, and for most Jews today the state of Israel is perceived as an essential bulwark against aggression, hatred and violence: Jews worldwide believe that Jews must protect themselves from assault. This was the theme of Theodor Herzl's *The Jewish State*, the classic work of secular Zionism. In Herzl's view, the building of a Jewish homeland in Palestine would transform Jewish life.

In the preface to his work, Herzl stated that his advocacy of a Jewish state was not simply a utopian scheme; on the contrary his plan was a realistic proposal arising out of the appalling conditions facing Jews living under oppression and persecution. Old prejudices against Jewry, he argued, are ingrained in Western society – assimilation will not act as a cure for the ills that beset the Jewish people. Only by creating a state in which they will be the majority, will the Jewish people be able to survive. By championing the concept of a Jewish refuge from persecution, Herzl laid the foundations for the creation of a Jewish homeland in the Middle East.

There is thus a tension in modern Judaism between the messianic longing for peace, and the recognition that we Jews live in a world where we have been and continue to be under attack. The Messianic Age has not dawned. In the shadow of the Holocaust, Jews are determined to ensure their survival. They insist that never again will their fate hang in the balance as it did under Nazi rule.

Dawoud   I think that George has identified a key point when he says that an unjust outcome in armed conflict is a cue for further hostilities. It is probably true to say, however, that in almost all conflict there will be injustice or perceived injustice which may perpetuate hostilities or continue to simmer below the surface when order is restored, only to boil over at a later date. Dan talks about the Jewish people's need after centuries of persecution to create a national home in which Jews would be able to live in peace and security, and this is entirely understandable. The problem is, however, that as a result of this an injustice has been perpetrated against the people of the land in which they have built their sanctuary and this has had repercussions up to the present.

I do not want simply to rehearse here the arguments in the Palestinian–Israeli conflict, which I have never considered to be religious but purely a matter of justice and equal humanity. Ultimately the causes of all wars and hostilities are the survival, protection and advancement of our own communities and societies and war is rarely wholly in the name of a religious cause. It may, however, become the call that rallies the oppressed and the dispossessed and those who seek redress in the case of injustice. From the late 19th and early 20th centuries, revivalist movements in Islam such as the Muslim Brotherhood arose as a focus of identity in the face of colonialism and external interference in the Islamic countries, as well as unjust rule by their own rulers and governments. For decades they were kept down by mainly secular governments until popular discontent allowed them to emerge. Anger at what was perceived to be effectively American rule via Mohammad Reza Shah Pahlavi as a puppet ruler led to the Islamic Revolution in Iran in 1979. In Afghanistan the Taliban started out as a resistance movement to the occupying Soviet forces.

More recently, there was anger at Western invasion and occupation of Iraq, in which a culturally and educationally sophisticated country with a high standard of living was devastated by bombing campaigns that took scant regard of civilian casualties. Iraq was then made to pay for its rebuilding with its own oil that had been locked down by a 10-year embargo following the first invasion. There is also a perception that Western powers have been responsible for providing support for brutal and corrupt Arab regimes such as that of al-Assad in Syria. This has led to a resurgence of a political Islam that is seeking to take back control from foreign powers and from its own corrupt leaders and to create a new Islamic caliphate. The rise of ISIS has caught everyone, including Muslims, by surprise. Supported by a highly sophisticated propaganda and recruitment network, it has been able to attract volunteers from around the world with the belief that they are fighting for a just cause and the promise of divine reward in the hereafter. While faith has the power to inspire the very best in people, it is also possible for those with a political agenda to select textual evidence and distort it to produce justifications for the worst possible behaviour and treatment of their opponents, rivals and even of their own people, and this is what we have seen in recent months.

George   Dawoud says that 'war is rarely wholly in the name of a religious cause' and provides some helpful political analysis of Middle Eastern affairs. However, Dan's comments highlight the religious rationale that underlies the Jews' desire for a homeland, and I find much of what he says quite disturbing. Dan writes as if he is presenting an uncontentious account of Jewish history, but – apart from a small handful of Christian fundamentalists – Christian scholarship seriously questions the historical veracity of the first six books of the Bible, which culminate in the invasion of Jericho.

The events described in the Torah purport to go back to around the 13th century BCE. The narrative, in all probability, was not committed to writing until the 8th and 9th centuries BCE, and not edited into its present form until the 7th or 6th centuries BCE. There is little external corroboration of the events described, and they are not historical records as modern historians would recognise. What historian recounts key figures as having extensive conversations with God, as Abraham and Moses appear to have, the miraculous protection of God's people, angels appearing with flaming swords, and Jericho's city walls falling down as a consequence of priests blowing trumpets? There are anachronisms and dubious statistics. The Ten Commandments mention 'the stranger who is within your gates' (Exodus 20:10). Did the ancient Israelites carry a set of city gates through the desert, to find that they fitted the city of Jericho, where they could finally use them? The Exodus story states that 600,000 Israelites were enslaved in Egypt (Exodus 12:37). This is the equivalent of the entire population of a modern city. (The population of Jericho, where they arrived, is around 18,500 today.)

It is more likely that the Torah recounts a set of folk tales which were devised to provide an identity for the Jewish people. But the nature of this identity lies at the root of the continued conflicts between the Jews and other nations throughout their history. The stories serve to legitimate the view that they are God's chosen people, the recipients of a special divine covenant which was not offered to other nations, and that their military conquests are not due to human strategies, but to divine victory won on their behalf.

We could have a debate about miracles at this juncture, but this take us beyond the present topic. Even if we were to allow that such things are possible, the story of Joshua's invasion of Jericho is surely not to the Jews' credit. Dan presents the Jews as an oppressed minority, and appeals to the 'shadow of the Holocaust' to reinforce this notion. Whatever happened to Moses and the Israelites in Egypt, they certainly do not seem to be a small persecuted group by the time they reach Jericho. The Bible states that they 'destroyed with the sword every living thing in it – men and women, young and old, cattle, sheep and donkeys' (Joshua 6:21). This sounds pretty much like genocide to me – hardly the action of an oppressed minority.

The acceptance of this biblical narrative lies behind much of the problem between Jews and Palestinians today. Taken literally, the Hebrew scriptures present a conquest narrative, a holy war, and a theology of land, which continues to legitimate modern conflicts. The fact that Christian fundamentalists also buy into this account – particularly in the United States – makes for a lethal political mêlée.

Dan George is right about the historicity of the biblical account. Archaeology has demonstrated that the Hebrew Scriptures are often unreliable. There is no evidence, for example, that the Jews were freed from Egyptian bondage, nor that the conquest of the Canaanites took place as depicted in the Book of Joshua. In essence we cannot reconstruct the history of the Jewish people in ancient times with any certainty. This does not mean, however, that we know nothing of the Jewish past. On the contrary, while we cannot determine with accuracy the early history of the Jewish people, there is much we do know. For example, in the British Museum there are artefacts such as the Black Obelisk of Shalmaneser III depicting tribute being paid by Jehu, king of Israel to the Assyrian king in the 9th century BCE as well as bas-reliefs of the conquest of the ancient city of Lachish by the Assyrians in the 8th century BCE that give us concrete information about ancient Jewish history. Remains of the ancient Temple in Jerusalem also provide confirmation of the biblical account of worship in ancient Israel.

What we have then is a blurred picture of ancient Jewish history: much of what the Bible tells us is inaccurate or has no evidential foundation. But, on the other hand, archaeology has confirmed the historicity of some events recorded in the Hebrew Bible. What George fails to perceive is that the account of Jewish history I gave earlier in this chapter is largely true. We cannot know exactly what took place at the earliest times in the history of the Jewish nation, but what we can say with certainty is that Jews were conquered and ruled over by foreign powers in ancient times. The Assyrians conquered the Kingdom of Israel in the 8th century BCE;

the Babylonians devastated the Kingdom of Judah in the 6th century BCE; and the Jewish nation in subsequent centuries was ruled over by the Seleucids, the Ptolemies and the Romans. In the 1st century CE a revolt against Roman rule was crushed, Jerusalem was destroyed, the Temple was demolished and Jews were led in captivity back to Rome. The Arch of Titus in Rome depicts these captives carrying a menorah in defeat.

For nearly twenty centuries the Jews have been in exile from their ancient homeland, and there are ample historical records which give us a detailed picture of Jewish suffering and persecution. Some years ago I wrote a book entitled *The Crucified Jew: Twenty Centuries of Christian Antisemitism* (2014) in which I traced the ways in which we Jews have been treated mercilessly by Christians over two millennia. During this long period of history, Jews were victims of hatred and violence. This is not fiction – it is fact. Our suffering gave rise to the Zionist conviction that Jews will never be secure as long as we are a minority people. The only solution to the problem of antisemitism is for Jewry to have its own country.

This is the background to the emergence of the state of Israel in modern times. The early Zionist pioneers had hoped that a Jewish settlement in Palestine would be acceptable to the indigenous Arab population, but this was not to be. From the first few decades of the 20th century until today, the Arab world refused to accept a Jewish homeland in Palestine and has been determined to drive the Jews into the sea. It is for this reason that Jews have armed themselves in the struggle for survival. After two millennia of being the victims of violence, we have been compelled to resort to war to defend ourselves from hostile aggression.

CHAPTER 4

Other forms of violence

There are different kinds of violence, and in the course of their history our three faiths have prescribed penalties for misdeeds, ranging from parental physical punishment to state executions. In recent times much media publicity has been given to beheadings by ISIS terrorists. How do our faiths view physical punishment?

Dan   So far we have been discussing war and peace in our three traditions. But we are concerned about the use of violence in other contexts and hence I want to turn to the issue of capital punishment. According to the Jewish tradition, there are four methods of capital punishment: stoning, burning, decapitation and strangulation. The 12th century Jewish philosopher, Moses Maimonides, listed the various crimes that merited such punishment in the Mishneh Torah, Sanhedrin, Chapter 15. They include:

(1)   Punishment by stoning for:

- Intercourse between a man and his mother

- Intercourse between a man and his father's wife

- Intercourse between a man and his daughter-in-law

- Intercourse between two men

- Bestiality

- Cursing the name of God in God's name

- Idol worship

- Witchcraft

- Violating the Sabbath

- Cursing one's parent

- A stubborn or rebellious son.

(2)   Punishment by burning for:

- Intercourse between a man and his daughter

- Intercourse between a man and his daughter's daughter

- Intercourse between a man and his wife's daughter

- Intercourse between a man and his mother-in-law

- Intercourse between a man and his father-in-law's mother.

(3)   Punishment by beheading for:

- Unlawful premeditated murder.

(4)   Punishment by strangulation for:

- Wounding one's own parent

- Kidnapping another member of Israel

- Prophesying in the name of other deities.

The harshness of the death penalty indicated the seriousness of a crime. Some Jewish philosophers argued that the point of corporeal punishment was to serve as a reminder to the community of the severe nature of the acts involved. Yet, the standards of proof required for the application of the death penalty were incredibly high. Such conditions as the following had to be fulfilled:

(1)   Two witnesses must observe the crime.

(2)   These witnesses had to be adult observant Jewish men.

(3)   The witnesses had to see each other at the time of the sin.

(4)   The witnesses could not be related to one another.

(5)   The witnesses had to give a warning to the person that the sin they were about to commit was a capital offence.

(6)   A warning had to be delivered within seconds of the performance of the act.

(7)   The person committing the act had to respond that he or she was familiar with the punishment but was going to sin anyway.

Because of these stringent rules, it was essentially impossible to inflict the death penalty. As a result, the Sanhedrin stopped pronouncing capital punishment either after the Second Temple was destroyed in 70 CE or later in 30 CE when the Sanhedrin was moved out of the Hall of Hewn Stones. Maimonides himself stated that it is better and more satisfactory to acquit a thousand guilty persons than to put a single innocent one to death.

In modern times Orthodox rabbis tend to hold the view that the death penalty is a correct and just punishment in theory, but they maintain that it should not be used in practice. Rabbinic courts have thus surrendered the ability to inflict any kind of physical punishment – such punishments are left to the civil court system to administer.

Since 1959 the Central Conference of American Rabbis (CCAR) has formally opposed the death penalty. The CCAR resolved in 1979 that both in concept and in practice, Jewish tradition found capital punishment repugnant and there is no persuasive evidence that capital punishment serves as a deterrent to crime. Conservative Judaism has gone on record as opposing the modern institution of the death penalty.

George   War and terrorism are the most obvious assaults on peace, as well as the most harmful, but there are many other forms of violence: capital and corporal punishment (as Dan mentions), suicide, abortion, domestic violence, even self-harm. Depending on how wide a definition of violence we adopt, experimentation on animals and harming the environment could also be considered as forms of violence.

Some of the classical Christian teachings shed light on some of these problems, particularly the doctrines of incarnation and redemption. Although some theologians have treated these as puzzles to be solved, they are perhaps better viewed as ways of highlighting aspects of human life. God's becoming human in the form of Jesus Christ shows that God has sanctified humanity, and considered human beings worth redeeming. No human being should be written off as incapable of being rescued, however hard this may be to believe in practice.

If such concepts sound sanctimonious, they can be expressed in more secular vocabulary: 'respect for persons', 'respect for life' or 'human dignity'. Involving innocent parties in conflicts (for example, by taking hostages) or using other human beings solely for one's own ends (as in slavery or human trafficking) are serious human rights violations.

Treating human beings with dignity must, of course, be compatible with the wider needs of society and the rights of others. Jesus' teaching that we should love our neighbours as ourselves implies that loving oneself (although not unduly privileging oneself) is legitimate. Self-defence is therefore acceptable for defending one's life or one's property. Offenders require punishment for deterrence and for public safety, but sanctions should be proportionate, employing the minimum force and suffering. Causing undue fear, needless violence or humiliation (for example, by torture, mock executions or public pillorying) goes against the idea of humans having been created in God's image. Whether capital punishment is a deterrent is debatable, but it continues to be practised in numerous US states, where Christianity is the dominant religion.

Dan mentions corporal punishment. When I was schooled in Scotland, the 'tawse' was occasionally used, and we all accepted it as a means of enforcing appropriate behaviour. However, societal attitudes have moved on, and it is not usually considered acceptable to use physical force on children any more. A number of Christian fundamentalists still believe in physical punishment, citing passages mainly from the book of Proverbs, such as 'Whoever spares the rod hates their children, but the one who loves their children is careful to discipline them' (Proverbs 13:24).

I hope that in what follows Dawoud will explain something about Muslim attitudes to physical punishment. Recently the journalist Raif Badawi was condemned to ten years imprisonment and 1,000 lashes in Saudi Arabia, for allegedly insulting Islam. Earlier in 2015 there were press reports of a victim of a violent gang rape – not the perpetrators – being condemned to receive 200 lashes. The Qur'an seems to teach that a husband may beat his wife if he believes that she is arrogant: 'advise them; [then if they persist], forsake them in bed; and [finally], strike them' (4:34).

Of course Christianity is not guilt free. There has been the Spanish Inquisition and the burning of heretics at the stake. King Henry VIII, who proclaimed himself head of the Church of England, had two of his wives beheaded. I think Christians have made progress since then. What about Islam?

Dawoud   Every violent act of whatever kind, whether lawful or unlawful, adds to the sum total of violence in a society and the degree to which human beings become inured to it and to the reporting of it.

In Islam there are indeed prescribed physical penalties for certain serious crimes. There is a body of penal law in the Shari'a known as the *hudud,* dealing with those acts that are deemed to be offences against God, including theft, extramarital sex of any kind, false accusation of illicit sex, consumption of alcohol, apostasy and highway robbery. Notwithstanding the argument as to whether some of the *hadd* offences should constitute crimes in the first place, in most Muslim countries which have enjoyed more than a century of civil society and legal reform and which have constitutions, codified legislation including penal codes, and strong judiciaries, we find that offences, including *hudud,* are dealt with through ordinary criminal courts with civil penalties including fines and custodial sentences. By contrast, under Shari'a law, the penalty for murder is in theory based on retribution and the family of the victim may accept bloodwit from the perpetrator or his or her family in order to avert a capital sentence, whereas under the penal codes of many Muslim countries the penalty for premeditated murder is death.

At the time of writing, the Middle East and other parts of the Islamic world are in turmoil and every day we hear of brutal executions and cruel and ghastly punishments meted out to people who appear in the eyes of any rational person to have done little, or more often nothing, to deserve any kind of punishment. There have even been cases where people, usually women, who in any civilised community would be considered to be victims, have been punished for adultery or fornication when in fact they have been raped. Some of these are state punishments, notably in the two great Islamic theocracies Saudi Arabia and Iran, the homelands of Sunni and Shi'i Islam, respectively. George refers to the case of Raif Badawi, sentenced to 1,000 lashes for insulting Islam although in fact he had only spoken out against the system in a country where interpretation of the law is in the hands of and at the personal discretion of religious scholars who derive their rulings directly from the applicable school of jurisprudence. This is without doubt an act of terror intended to make an example of him and thereby to suppress other dissenting voices.

The most appalling so-called Islamic punishments that we have seen in recent years have been the actions of self-styled regimes and militias where self-appointed judges and councils operate without the checks and balances of a stable society. Using their distorted interpretations of the Shari'a, they are able to settle scores and maintain a reign of fear and to establish a culture of misogyny that has set back the position of women in parts of the Islamic world by more than a hundred years. This situation has also given individuals the opportunity to act as vigilantes and to exert power arbitrarily over life and death. It is impossible to see such actions as anything other than a form of terror.

Dan So far we have been discussing various types of violence perpetrated in the name of our three faiths. But we have not said much about the issue of terror. In recent years terrorism has been condemned throughout the world. Terrorists are vilified in the press and castigated by religious leaders. In particular, Islamic terrorism sponsored by jihadists is vehemently denounced.

Yet it has to be admitted that in the past acts of terrorism have been unleashed by members of our faith communities in pursuit of religious and political aims. Modern Jewish history bears witness to armed attack on innocent victims in the struggle to create a Jewish state. The bombing of the King David Hotel, for example, was an attack carried out on 22 July 1946 by the militant underground organisation, the Irgun, on the British headquarters housed in the King David Hotel in Jerusalem. Ninety-one people of various nationalities were killed and 46 were injured. In the House of Commons, Prime Minister Clement Atlee stated:

Hon. Members will have learned with horror of the brutal and murderous crime committed yesterday in Jerusalem. Of all the outrages which have occurred in Palestine, and they have been many and horrible in the last few months, this is the worst. (House of Commons Debates, Hansard 425:1877–78, 23 July 1946)

Later in the Palestinian–Israeli conflict, the massacre that took place in the Sabra and Shatila refugee camps resulted in the killing of between 762 and 3,500 civilians by a Christian Lebanese right-wing party. At the time of this slaughter, the Israeli army surrounded the refugee camps and stationed troops at the exits of the areas to prevent camp residents from fleeing.

In the light of these and other acts of murderous slaughter, both the Jewish and Christian communities should not regard themselves as free from criticism. Yet there is no doubt that around the world Islamic jihadists feel fully justified in using terrorism on a massive scale to achieve their political and religious ends. Today ISIS is unapologetic about using extreme violence. Daily we are witnesses to a murderous rampage across the Middle East.

Determined to establish a caliphate there and elsewhere, its followers insist on the implementation of strict Shari'a law. Islamic State's leadership believe they are on course for an apocalyptic battle with their enemies from which they will emerge victorious. They foretell that non-Islamic forces will mass to meet the armies of Islam in northern Syria, and that Islam's final showdown will occur in Jerusalem after a period of Islamic conquest.

Is such a vision truly Islamic? This is the question I want to ask Dawoud. Islamic State claims to be the sole representative of Islam and has executed large numbers of Muslims whose understanding of the Qur'an differs from theirs. Is ISIS is a misrepresentation of true Islamic values? If so, why are its believers convinced they are following Allah?

Given the long histories of bloodshed in our three traditions, how are we to differentiate between legitimate acts of violence? What do we mean by terrorism? Is it always wrong? In the deadly conflicts engulfing the world, who are the freedom fighters? Who are the terrorists? Where is evil to be found?

George The word 'terrorist' is highly pejorative, and of course it is intended to be. Dan cites a number of examples, but I think we need to take a step back and consider the complexity of the term. The public often engage in 'tabloid thinking', making remarks like, 'It all started with 9/11' – as if the bombing of the World Trade Center had no background. We have all heard the aphorism that 'one person's terrorist is another person's freedom fighter', and although this has become a cliché, it highlights the point that terrorists have a cause, which they regard as worth pursuing and even dying for.

There is no agreed definition of terrorism, and the United Nations has been unable to arrive at a legal definition. To suggest, for example, that a terrorist pursues an unworthy cause overlooks the possibility that one's cause might be just but one's methods of attaining it unacceptable. Terrorism is frequently associated with ideological rather than religious aims, but politics and religion are intertwined, and in the next chapter we shall discuss the extent to which it is possible to disentangle the two, and whether religions typically teach or provoke violence.

Terrorism is often associated with small groups of combatants who are not authorised to fight by a state. However, states themselves have sometimes been described as terrorist when they oppress minorities, use methods of torture, or conduct mass executions. The term 'Reign of Terror' was first used to refer to the French government of 1793–1794. In 2014 Bolivian President Evo Morales applied the term 'terrorist state' to Israel, renouncing a visa exemption agreement on account of its military offensive in Gaza. He said, 'Israel is not a guarantor of the principles of respect for life and the elementary precepts of rights that govern the peaceful and harmonious coexistence of our international community' (*Arutz Sheva*, 30 July 2014).

Terrorist organisations, unlike terrorist states, tend to be small by comparison. If they were to oppose an enemy state as a traditional army, wearing clearly identifiable uniforms and in open combat, they would certainly be defeated. They therefore have to resort to alternative methods of hostility, engaging in violent acts that induce fear, killing or maiming civilians, taking hostages, and thus gaining high media publicity for their cause. The level of security checks to which international travellers are subjected shows how effective they are in instilling fear.

Although security precautions were stepped up after 9/11, the bombing of the World Trade Center was certainly not 'the start', although the background is not wholly clear. There are different theories about Al-Qaeda. Some believe that Osama bin Laden wanted to counter a supposed Christian–Jewish alliance which sought to destroy Islam. Others have suggested that the organisation or network aims to counter the splintering of Islam which has occurred in the course of history, making it a single unified regime. Another explanation is that bin Laden wanted to provoke the foreign invasion of an Islamic country, while a further theory is that Al-Qaeda wanted to make its mark against US military and economic power.

Terrorism, however defined, has a background and purpose. This is not to condone it or excuse it, but to highlight the need to understand it. The question we need to pose is: Who are the real terrorists? Are they cells of guerrilla fighters, or are they provoked by state terrorism?

Dawoud   As both Dan and George have pointed out, members of all our faiths have been responsible for acts of barbarism perpetrated not only against each other but also against members of their own religions who hold opinions that differ from their own. Dan discusses the acts of terror perpetrated by the Israeli militias, such as the bombing of the King David Hotel. This was designed to drive the British out of Palestine and in this it was completely successful, but there was also a campaign of terror on a much greater scale aimed at driving Palestinians from their homes and lands. These include the massacre at the village of Deir Yassin in 1948, which sent a message of terror. This led to the flight of thousands of Palestinians who, once removed, were never able to return to their homes and villages and have remained stateless ever since. Throughout the history of the conflict between Palestinians and Israelis, both sides have committed atrocities, but it has to be remembered that Israel is a state with vast military resources that have enabled it to impose its might, backed up by a highly effective propaganda machine that has allowed it to impress its point of view on the media and public opinion worldwide. The scale of destruction of Palestinian life and property by Israel far outweighs the damage done to Israel by Palestinians, yet somehow Palestinian lives are considered less important than those of Israelis.

What we are seeing at the moment in the horror of ISIS is the effect of propaganda supercharged with the power of social media. ISIS does not represent all Muslims and most ordinary people worldwide are horrified by its acts of terror. It does not represent them any more than Hitler represented all Christians, or than the Communist regimes represented all their citizens; yet ISIS holds its followers and those around them in thrall by a combination of fear and conviction in a distorted ideology. ISIS is a totalitarian regime that tolerates no dissent and uses its narrow interpretation of the faith as a blunt instrument, justifying the most appalling behaviour. Yet totalitarian regimes do not come out of nowhere. They are most often the product of a profound dissatisfaction with the existing regime which may be perceived to be corrupt and unjust and to have no moral authority to rule. In Syria, as in many parts of the Arab world, longstanding resentment of brutal authoritarian governments and foreign exploitation opened the door to resistance which has gone on to take the form of a much more brutal dictatorship. As with other totalitarian regimes, ISIS has terrorised many people into compliance as a way of simply keeping themselves and their families alive, yet at the same time they are appealing to Muslims in other parts of the Muslim world and the West with a simplistic and absolutist message, claiming to be the only true representatives of the faith working for the establishment of a worldwide Islamic caliphate. As such they have gained a following facilitated by social media and using grooming methods not entirely unlike those used by paedophiles who prey upon the vulnerable and suggestible.

CHAPTER 5

Does religion cause violence?

Unsympathetic critics, such as Richard Dawkins and the 'new atheists', often accuse religion of doing more harm than good, claiming that religion is at the root of most of the war and violence in the world. In this chapter we examine the role of religion in terror, violence and war.

George   In his bestseller, *The God Delusion*, Richard Dawkins blames religion for all kinds of violence: war, acts of terrorism, executions, violence against women, racism, paedophilia, environmental harm, cruel sports and much more. *The World Factbook* of the CIA reports the results of a 2010 survey which estimates that a mere 2.01% of the world's population are atheists, and 9.66% are non-religious (Central Intelligence Agency, 2015). It is therefore not surprising that most acts of violence are carried out by people who claim some kind of religious affiliation. However, this does not mean that 'religion' is the cause of violence. A country like North Korea, which is sometimes said to be 100% atheist, scarcely inspires confidence that atheists are more peace-loving than their religious counterparts, and Pol Pot's genocide in Cambodia in the 1970s was aimed at securing a type of communist regime.

In common with the average member of the public, Dawkins seems to write as if religion were a 'thing' that is clearly identifiable and separate from other kinds of activity. Not only do scholars of religion continue to argue about what exactly religion is, but religious beliefs and activities are not separate from other aspects of everyday living, such as ethics, politics, economics, health, earning a living and, of course, peace and violence. To blame religion for terror, war and violence is to single out one strand of human behaviour to the exclusion of others. One could equally argue that politics is the cause of violence, since politicians decide our defence budgets, and terrorist groups have political goals. Science and technology could just as readily be argued to share the blame, since guns and bombs were developed through technological expertise. The armaments manufacturers must share some responsibility for the world's violence.

It is important to distinguish different types of armed conflict in which religious people engage. First, there have been wars whose purpose has been to displace one religion with another, although this is not so common today. ISIS may be a case in point, seeking as it does to establish a theocratic state, with a caliph who is believed to be a successor of Muhammad. Second, there have been wars for national defence, or for political or ideological goals, which have been sanctioned by religious leaders. Throughout its history, Christian leaders have sanctioned participation in war where the cause was perceived as just.

Third, there have been conflicts in which the different parties have belonged to different forms of religion, but where opposition has only been tangentially about religious differences. Hitler's attempt to exterminate Jews was not primarily because of their religion, although he alleged that their Sabbath observance was inconvenient in German society – his declared reason was based on spurious evolutionary biological arguments. No Jew could escape the death camps by converting to Christianity. (As a disciple of Darwin, Dawkins might profitably consider whether evolutionary theory could be a cause of violence!)

It is problematic to contend that something is done 'in the name of religion'. If we are religious, there is an important sense in which anything we do bears the name of our faith. Paul said that Christians are 'Christ's ambassadors' (2 Corinthians 5:20), and others judge the Christian faith by what they see us do. But this does not mean that we are acting on behalf of our religion, or even being faithful practitioners of its teachings. Are ISIS supporters ambassadors for Islam, or are they the antithesis of faithful Muslims?

Dawoud   I think that Richard Dawkins is as entitled to hold his worldview unmolested, as are any of the rest of us, but I am inclined to agree with

George that it is not religion as such that is the cause of armed conflict or other acts of violence, any more than guns are the cause of armed robbery or murder, or even war. However much one may detest the American gun lobby, there is some truth in their justification that 'Guns don't kill people, people kill people'. The problem is that guns, like religions, can fall into the wrong hands. If they are not treated with respect, understanding and caution, they create a sense of power, and enable those who carry them to impose their own opinions, interests and agendas, however essentially immoral, aggressive or even psychopathic these may be. The metaphor breaks down here, as there is a very strong argument for restricting the possession of firearms, but there is no valid case for restricting what people may or may not believe. In both cases, however, there is a moral imperative to provide people with information and education about the dangers that beliefs, like guns, may present.

So, religion doesn't start wars; people start wars. People of religion do not engage in violence or initiate armed conflict for the sake of religion unless they are driven by other factors, either offensive or defensive. These may include competition for space or scarce resources, material opportunism or territorial expansion, injustice or perceived injustice or oppression, and resistance to external aggression or invasion. It is, however, easy for leaders, legitimate or self-styled, to dress up a political or military agenda in the guise of religion, thereby claiming ultimate and unchallengeable moral authority, and ensuring the maximum level of commitment and even the willingness of their followers to sacrifice their own lives and to take those of others.

George mentions that Christian leaders have at times sanctioned participation in war, but sometimes they have actively promoted it. The Crusades drew on religious fervour for recruitment for campaigns that were motivated as much by economic and political expansionist aims. The Irish 'Troubles' were and are complex and deep rooted based on old grievances but manifested in an intractable inter-denominational conflict that can be traced back to Henry VIII's breakaway from the political and economic domination of Rome. Jews have a valid reason for seeking a place where they can live free from persecution, but some, although by no means all, have justified their colonisation of Palestine, and have been supported in this by some Christian groups, on the grounds of ancient scripture and the notion that they are God's chosen people with an absolute right to the Land of Israel in perpetuity. The Iranian Revolution took up the flag of Shi'i Islam as the standard of resistance to US political and economic denomination and exploitation. ISIS, likewise, is in part the reaction to the way that Western powers have ridden roughshod over the Middle East over the last century. This in no way justifies their actions, which do not represent the views of the majority of Muslims worldwide, or the opinions of the majority of the religious authorities. They do, however, make a simplistic literalist case for their actions that is easy to market to the disaffected and dispossessed but which bypasses 1,400 years of cultural diversity and intellectual and spiritual tradition.

Dan In your two exchanges, you have challenged Richard Dawkins' contention that religion is the primary cause of war. George stressed that religion cannot be separated out from other factors that motivate human action. Dawoud used the metaphor of a gun causing violence, to emphasise that what matters is who pulls the trigger. Guns, he points out, often fall into the wrong hands.

Academic studies have similarly challenged the link between religion and war. The *Encyclopaedia of Wars*, published in 2008, catalogued 1,763 wars throughout human history, and concluded that just 123 were religious in nature. Research published by the Institute for Economics and Peace looked at all wars that took place in 2013, and concluded that they found no general causal relationship between religion and conflict. Religious elements played no role at all in 14 (40%) of the 35 armed conflicts described in the research, and only 5 (14%) had religious elements as their central cause. All the wars had multiple causes, and the much more common factor was opposition to a government, or to the economic, ideological, political or social systems of a state. This was named as a main factor in nearly two thirds of the cases studied. The Institute report also concluded that having less religion in a country does not make it more peaceful. Countries with the highest levels of atheism were not necessarily the most peaceful. North Korea, for example, has one of the lowest rates of people practising religion, yet it is one of the least peaceful countries in the world (Ridley, 2014).

As you both have pointed out, the reality of armed conflict is usually complex even if wars are fought in the name of religion. Often factors such as dynastic influence, power and economics are of central significance. A much more realistic appraisal is that religion is implicated in many conflicts. In her recent book, *Fields of Blood: Religion and the History of Violence*, Karen Armstrong argues that the Western word 'religion' cannot be accurately translated into non-Western cultures. While the West regards faith as a personal matter, in the East – and this has been so for most of human history – it is inseparable from politics. Hence, it is a mistake to maintain, as do Dawkins and others, that religion can be separated out as the primary factor causing human conflict.

Nonetheless, there is no doubt that religious belief has been a significant element in fuelling hatred, persecution, violence and war throughout history even if it is not the sole or main factor. Let me cite just one example. During the Inquisition in Spain in the 15th century torture was frequently used to extract confessions from conversos (Jewish converts). Typical procedures used by the Inquisitors are seen in the case of Elvira del Campo who was accused by the authorities of Judaizing. She was carried to the torture chamber and told to tell the truth. Her arms were tied, and the pressure increased in intensity. Eventually, she was set upon the rack. In Spain and later in Portugal, the judicial sentence of the Inquisitors following such torture was passed in public in the presence of dignitaries and crowds. Hundreds of thousands of people were charged and over 30,000 suffered the death penalty. The Inquisition was not carried out by a rogue institution of the Christian faith, rather, it was official Roman Catholic policy. This is a simple example of human cruelty motivated by religious fervour. Even if religion is cleared of Dawkins' charge of being the main cause of human suffering, we must still face the fact that our faiths have been implicated in terror, violence and war.

George Monty Python enthusiasts will no doubt recall the Spanish Inquisition sketch in which fully robed cardinals burst into improbable situations shouting, 'No one expects the Spanish Inquisition!' It would be truer, however, to say that no one *forgets* the Spanish Inquisition, not least Dan here, and of course Richard Dawkins in his *The God Delusion*.

Most religions have their Hall of Shame, but it is important to see things in perspective. The Spanish Inquisition investigated 125,000 persons, and probably executed slightly more than 2,000 (somewhat fewer than

Dan alleges). Compare that with Pol Pot's Khmer Rouge, which caused the deaths of somewhere between 1.7 and 2.5 million people between 1970 and 1987 – around 21% of Cambodia's population – an atrocity committed in the name of a secular ideology. Of course these are two selected instances, but it does not inspire confidence that secular ideology fares any better in respecting human rights and welfare than religions. Interestingly, Dawkins does not refer to Pol Pot. Of course we cannot draw up a balance sheet for the good and harm caused by religion and non-religion. Not only are good and harm unquantifiable (apart from statistics such as death tolls) but, as I suggested previously, religion is not a 'thing' from which good and harm emanate.

Atrocities occur in the history of most religions. By and large, the Christian faith has moved beyond the Inquisition and, just as I would want to dissociate Christianity from the Inquisition, I hope that Dan would equally condemn the Jewish genocides involved in the invasion of Jericho (Joshua 6:21), King Saul's massacre of the Amalekites, in which only the king and a few cattle were spared (1 Samuel 15:8), and the various Israelite kings' murders of the Baal prophets. I am sure that Dawoud, equally, would not want to associate Islam with Ayatollah Khomeni or Saddam Hussein.

However, I wonder why discussions like this always home in on the atrocities. Surely we need to remind ourselves that religions have actually done good, and have contributed to peace. In the course of history, over forty popes have had a mediatorial role, helping to negotiate treaties that have brought armed conflicts to an end. Perhaps the best known is Pope Leo I, who negotiated in 452 CE with Attila the Hun, who was dissuaded from invading Rome. Quite apart from war and peace, Christianity has had an important role in founding hospitals, clinics and educational institutions, has set up counselling and relief organisations, and has worked to combat slavery, racism, alcohol and gambling addiction, and many other human maladies.

As far as war is concerned, religion has had no role in most modern major wars. The two world wars were not fought for any religious cause, and conflicts such as the Korean War and the Vietnam War were ideological, and certainly not religious, conflicts. Most wars in fact are about resources, land or ideology.

No doubt our three faiths could do much better, but we should not allow our detractors to suggest that religion has done more harm than good. This is sheer ignorance and bigotry. Certainly religious people have done harm, and at times given their actions a religious justification, but, as Dawoud aptly says, it is religion in the wrong hands that can cause problems.

Dawoud   Steven Weinberg, a Nobel Prize winning physicist, has said of religion: 'With or without it you would have good people doing good things and evil people doing evil things, but for good people to do evil things, that takes religion' (*The New York Times*, 20 April 1999). I understand the point that he is making here and I think that there is some truth in it, but I do not think that the kind of motivation that he is referring to is necessarily related only to religion. I think we could replace the word 'religion' with 'ideology' as we only have to look at the atrocities perpetrated in the mid-20th century in the name of communism, itself a system founded on a reaction to injustice and oppression and the desire to create a fairer and more just society.

I think we are all agreed that religion itself is very rarely the actual cause of conflict, but in so many cases it is deeply held belief and absolute commitment that leads people to join causes which are responsible for acts of violence and terrorism. The recruits to ISIS, mostly young people but even some whole families who have left the UK and other European countries to make their way to Syria to join Islamic State, are not evil people bent on murder and mayhem but idealists who genuinely believe that they are working to create a better world based on the principles of Islam as they see them. Very often their own families are the most shocked and horrified that their loved ones have been radicalised in this way.

The current situation in the Middle East has been a long time in the making. Throughout the region and elsewhere in the Islamic world, radical Islamic organisations have won hearts and minds by filling the gaps left by weak and corrupt governments and have presented people with the prospect of a fairer and more ethical way of life based on Qur'anic principles. In Egypt, for example, the Muslim Brotherhood has re-emerged from within the population where for years it has been propping up communities at a grassroots level with welfare, medical help, education and advice, while the official authorities have failed to give people hope of any kind of future. In Palestine and particularly in Gaza, after years of working within communities to support and defend the population, providing schools, clinics and financial aid on a basis of need, Hamas, an offshoot of the Brotherhood, was elected as the legitimate government of the Palestinian territories.

As George points out, in focusing on the current violent situation amid the crimes of the past it is easy to overlook the positive contributions of religion. Islam has a strong tradition of charity and social responsibility. One of the pillars of faith is a compulsory 4% annual tax on a person's wealth, which is to be used for poor relief. Muslims are encouraged to provide food for the needy, particularly at the times of the major feasts. Since the Middle Ages, Islamic foundations based on the institution of the waqf, a particular kind of Islamic property trust, have built public hospitals and schools and supported a range of charitable causes. There have also been major contributions to inter-communal peace and security. It was the Ottoman Caliphate, for example, which offered refuge to Jews expelled or fleeing from different parts of Christendom from the 14th century onwards and which allowed Jewish communities to prosper throughout its territories.

Dan In this chapter, we have been discussing whether religions are responsible for acts of violence. There is no doubt that all three of our faiths have in different ways been implicated in terror, violence and war despite the good that religion has achieved. We will need to explore in greater detail such involvement in later chapters. But I want to return to the serious questions George posed earlier about the nature of terrorism since it is so prominent in our discussions. The term comes from the French word *terrorisme*, which originally referred to state terrorism as practised by the French government during the 1793–1794 Reign of Terror. The French word *terrorisme* derives from the Latin verb *terreo* meaning 'I frighten'. Although terrorism originally referred to acts committed by a government, currently it usually refers to the killing of innocent people for political purposes to create a media spectacle.

In modern times there are a number of ways of understanding the term. In general terrorism is defined as a violent act intended to create fear; this is done for economic, religious, political or ideological reasons. It usually targets non-combatants as opposed to military personnel. Another common definition views terrorism as political, ideological or religious violence performed by non-state agents. An essential characteristic of these various definitions is the focus on violence perpetrated against the innocent. Normally terrorism is condemned as evil, yet its defenders contend that terrorists resort to violence in order to combat injustice. In this context, terrorists are viewed as freedom fighters. In some cases, state authorities resort to armed force targeting the innocent to achieve political ends. Such acts are no less terrorism, yet they are justified in terms of the ends achieved.

Not surprisingly there is no universally agreed definition of terrorism, and various legal systems and governmental agencies use different definitions of terrorism in their national legislation. Further, the international community has been slow to formulate a universally agreed definition of this crime. During the 1970s and 1980s, the United Nations attempted to define the term but failed. This was due to differences of opinion between various members about the use of violence in the context of conflicts over national liberation and self-determination. Nonetheless, since 1984 the United Nations General Assembly has condemned terrorist acts using this description:

> Criminal acts intended or calculated to provoke a state of terror in the public, a group of persons or particular persons for political purposes are in any circumstance unjustifiable. Whatever the considerations of a political, philosophical, racial, ethnic, religious or any other nature that may be invoked to justify them (1994 United Nations Declaration on Measures to Eliminate International Terrorism annex to UN General Assembly resolution 49/60; Measures to Eliminate International Terrorism, of 9 December 1994, UN Doc. A/Res/49/60)

Arguably, this is the definition of terrorism we should adhere to in this book.

The other issue I want to refer to is George's earlier question about the conquest of ancient Canaan by the Israelites. According to Scripture, the indigenous Canaanite population was devastated by the invading Hebrews. This was a bloody massacre in which men, women and children lost their lives at the hands of the invaders. The Book of Joshua describes the battles that took place in graphic detail. For some modern Israelis, the conquest of Canaan serves as a justification for Israel's policy towards the Palestinians today. In the view of these Jewish fundamentalists, God promised the Holy Land to the Jewish people. Hence, Jewry has an inalienable right to every inch of soil, stretching from the Nile to the Euphrates. In my view, this is a pernicious myth perpetrated by misguided Jewish fanatics, and a major hindrance to peace and reconciliation.

CHAPTER 6

Are all faiths equally guilty?

The media frequently associate Islam in particular with violence, speaking of 'Muslim fundamentalists' and 'Islamic extremists'. Are Muslims really worse than Jews and Christians. Have not all three faiths been responsible for bloodshed?

Dawoud If we are going to try to answer this question I think we first of all have to consider our terms of reference. As we have mentioned in earlier discussions, at various times in history, followers of all our faiths have committed acts of violence. But how do we score these? How do we measure relative levels of violence? How do we determine the extent to which they are motivated or justified by religious belief?

If we are looking specifically at levels of violence in our own times, it would be quite disingenuous to suggest that Islam is no more violent than the other religions as this is clearly not the case. Islamic extremists have been responsible for more acts of violence and terrorism in recent years than any other group and hardly a day goes by without reports of bombings, kidnappings, shootings of innocent parties or cruel executions and other barbaric punishments both in Muslim countries and in the West. Western countries are on alert regarding the possibility of bombs or terrorist attacks of the kind carried out on the London Underground in 2005, the attacks in Paris in November 2015 and the Brussels bombings in March 2016. This is not entirely new, however. Many people are too young to remember the fear under which the British public lived for a number of years in the 1970s and into the 1980s when the IRA planted bombs in pubs and shopping centres in British cities, when litter bins – which are ideal hiding places for explosive devices – disappeared from city centres and people got used to having their bags searched on entering department stores.

During the Irish 'Troubles', members of two Christian communities committed the most appalling acts of violence against each other and other innocent victims. On one level this was seen as a conflict between two religious factions, but it would not really be true to say that violence was purely religiously inspired, since the roots of the conflict were complex and the aims of the IRA and Sinn Féin, and of their Unionist opponents, were essentially political.

There have been Jewish terrorist organisations such as the Irgun and the Stern Gang which were the most active in the period leading up to the creation of the State of Israel. These were responsible for many atrocities, but they were not religiously motivated and many of their leaders were European secular socialists. Today there are communities of Orthodox Jewish settlers who are permitted to carry weapons and who sometimes used these against unarmed Palestinians. The worst such incident was the unprovoked 1994 attack by Baruch Goldstein which killed twenty-five people praying at the main mosque in Hebron.

All three faiths have their terrorists, but this does not make them terrorist religions. Although we are living at a time when acts of terror and violence by Muslims in the name of Islam are in the news every day, this does not mean that all or the majority of Muslims are violent themselves or support violence.

Dan   Dawoud is right: our three faiths are not guiltless of involvement in acts of violence. On an individual level, capital punishment has been advocated by our traditions for a number of crimes (although since biblical times Jews have not punished offenders in this way). Yet both Christians and Muslims have a much worse record than Jews when it comes to physical harassment, torture and armed conflict.

From the outset Islam has been a religion of the sword. At first Muhammad lived peacefully with the Jewish community, but he quickly became hostile to Jews and eliminated most of them from Medina by either expulsion, enslavement or death. In ensuing centuries fervent Muslims spread the message of the Prophet through armed conflict and conquest. The current situation is not an aberration, rather Muslims fighters intent on establishing Shari'a law and creating a caliphate through terror and war are acting in the same spirit as those who came before. ISIS is not a distortion of Islam but a logical outcome of deeply held religious principles.

Christianity, too, has triumphed through violent conflict. The Crusades were undertaken by the faithful, believing they were fulfilling God's will. The Inquisition was a religious response to the perceived threat of conversos who remained loyal to their ancestral faith. I mentioned previously that some years ago I wrote a book entitled *The Crucified Jew: Twenty Centuries of Christian Antisemitism* (2014) which chronicles 2,000 years of Christian contempt and hostility towards Jews and Judaism. For us the cross does not represent God's love of humanity, rather it is a symbol of Jewish suffering. It casts a dark shadow over our history as a minority group living in Christian lands.

It is true that in modern times Zionists have used violence to achieve their ends in the Holy Land. Prior to the establishment of a Jewish state, the Irgun and the Stern Gang deliberately targeted victims in the conflict with Arabs and the British. Some of these actions are reprehensible despite the threat to the Jewish pioneers. Subsequently, Israel has defended itself by creating a powerful military establishment. In the quest to ensure the survival of the Jewish state, Israel has at times been insensitive to the suffering of the indigenous Arab population. Today many Palestinians have become victims in this ongoing dispute. Yet, violent conflict has not been a central feature of Jewish history precisely because we Jews have until recent times never been a majority people. Instead we have been victims, powerless against those who hated us. Jewish history is awash with blood, but it is our blood.

George   I fear we may be running the risk of turning this into a competition! Dan clearly wants to present his own faith as having the best track record when it comes to terror and violence. However, some 33% of the world's population is Christian, 21% Muslim, and only 0.22% Jewish, so it would be interesting to reflect on whether our three faiths have perpetrated violence in these proportions.

Dan mentions once again the Spanish Inquisition and Christianity's poor track record regarding Jews. But religions change over time, and we should be encouraged that moral progress is possible. We no longer burn heretics at the stake, and the gross antisemitism of leaders such as John Chrysostom, Augustine, Jerome and Martin Luther has given way to documents such as Pope Paul VI's *Nostra Aetate* ('In Our Time'), which states that:

> what happened in [Christ's] passion cannot be charged against all the Jews, without distinction . . . The Jews should not be presented as rejected or accursed by God, as if this followed from the Holy Scriptures.

Christianity teaches the fundamental ideas of forgiveness and repentance, and I hope that Dan and Dawoud would agree that today's Christians should not be judged by Christianity's past.

The question posed in this chapter is whether our three religions are today equally guilty of violence. It continues to be disturbing that some Christian groups still use violence in the name of their religion. The National Liberation Front of Tripura in India uses violent means to force conversion. The Lord's Resistance Army seeks to rule Uganda according to the Ten Commandments, but ironically uses murder, kidnapping and child soldiers in pursuit of its goals. In Central Africa, the anti-balaka are vigilante groups supported by Christians (although also animists) and forcibly oppose Muslims.

In the United States the Army of God has been responsible for nail bomb and arson attacks on abortion clinics. In 2001 one member sent hundreds of letters to abortion providers containing a white powder which he claimed (falsely) to be anthrax. Then there are the Christian Identity organisations – white supremacist groups who violently oppose Jews, foreigners and homosexuals. The best-known of these, although not the largest, is the Ku Klux Klan, who are well known for their attacks on Jews and Roman Catholics. The (white supremacist) Montana Freemen attracted publicity in 1996 for their armed opposition to the federal authorities, seeking to establish their own independent Christian state. These organisations do not attract as much publicity as Irgun, the Stern Gang, Al-Qaeda and ISIS, no doubt because they tend to focus their violence on the objects of their hatred rather than the public at large. Since they do not terrorise at an international level, they do not impact to the same degree on our lives.

It is worrying that these groups turn to the Bible for support. White supremacists have sometimes claimed that Jews are the children of Satan, being the offspring of an illicit relationship between Eve and the serpent. (This is not quite what the Bible says!) Some have claimed that black people are the descendants of Noah's son Ham, who received God's curse (Genesis 9:20–27). Some Christian fundamentalists have taken the story of Joshua's invasion of Jericho – which belongs to Christian as well as Jewish scriptures – to justify violence against all false religion.

These groups are certainly an embarrassment. Most Christians want to disown them, and they certainly do not belong to mainstream ecumenical bodies like the World Council of Churches.

Dawoud   George is quite right – we could catalogue episodes of terror and violence and score them against each other, but how should we measure them? In numbers of men, women and children killed, maimed, displaced or traumatised? Does it make a difference whether they are military personnel, politicians or civilians; deliberate or random targets or collateral damage? Can we compare degrees of savagery, sadism or indifference? How do we calculate what proportion of the motive for an act of violence is religious and how much of it is political, economic or ethnic? I could, for instance, quote the relative numbers of killings of Israelis and Palestinians from September 2000 to the end of 2014 given by B'Tselem, The Israeli Centre for Human Rights in the Occupied Territories, which estimates that at least 1,196 Israelis and 9,137 Palestinians were killed during this period. The people killed included 129 Israeli and 1,523 Palestinian children, 731 Israeli and an unconfirmed number of between 3,535 and 4,226 Palestinian civilians, one Israeli and at least 408 Palestinians killed in targeted killings, 596 Israelis and 6,756 Palestinians killed on their own land, respectively, and 508 Israelis compared with 73 Palestinians killed on others' land.

What do these statistics tell us? They do not alter the fact that over the centuries Jews have been victims of violence and persecution, and they do not prove that Judaism is more violent than Islam, as Israelis are a heterogeneous society composed of an entire spectrum of people from the ultra-Orthodox to the secular and even atheist. The actions of the State of Israel are not dictated by religious doctrine but by the ultimate political will to defend the state and its population. It is notable that

Israel has gone to extraordinary lengths at times to find, ransom or rescue individual Israelis who have fallen captive to Palestinians, such as the 2011 release of over 1,000 prisoners in return for the freedom of Gilad Shabblit who had been held prisoner in a secret location in Gaza for more than five years. For Israel, rightly, this one life was precious and worth every effort to save, yet it seems not to hold Palestinian lives so valuable when inflicting wholly disproportionate violence on entire cities in Gaza, such as during Operation Protective Edge when more than 2,000 Gazans were killed and at least 100,000 injured as 20,000 homes were destroyed.

At the same time, it has to be acknowledged that there is a rapidly growing cult of martyrdom in Islam that places little or no value on the individual life, either of Muslims or non-Muslims, in this world and emphasises that the only life that really matters is in the hereafter. There is nothing in other faiths that compares with this literalist understanding of the Islamic doctrine of jihad which leads highly committed idealistic, mostly young, Muslims to believe they have no personal investment in the present and that the best way that they can serve God's will is to fight with the earnest hope that they may be killed in battle or even to sacrifice their lives in suicide missions that will transport them directly to Paradise. I maintain, however, that the majority of the world's perhaps two billion Muslims wish only to live in peace and prosperity.

Dan Contrary to Dawoud's view, I believe it is possible to compare our three faiths in relation to terror, war and violence. For nearly 2,000 years Christians persecuted and murdered Jews, and spread the Christian Gospel through coercion and force. In doing so, they ignored Jesus' message of love and peace. Similarly, Islam has from its inception been a religion of the sword, causing mayhem, destruction and death. ISIS is a contemporary manifestation of its will to power. Judaism, on the other hand, has until recent times not been in a position to conquer populations through armed conflict. Outside of Israel, Jews remain a small minority people living amidst majority populations.

In recent times, however, as Dawoud points out, the Jewish state has inflicted great hardship on Palestinians living in Gaza, the Occupied Territories and refugee camps. In this respect it mirrors the actions of Christians and Muslims through the ages. It can now exert its will against its enemies, causing misery and despair. This is the advantage of being a majority population in its own country.

Had Arabs accepted the early Jewish pioneers who settled in Palestine at the beginning of the 20th century, there could have been peaceful reconciliation between Jews and Muslims in the Holy Land. Instead, however, the indigenous population rose up against those they perceived as usurpers. Rejecting the Balfour Declaration, they embarked upon a holy crusade against Jewish inhabitants.

Understandably the early Zionists retaliated, intent on protecting Jewish lives from this onslaught and there ensued a series of bloody wars between Israel and its Arab neighbours. As Israel grew militarily stronger, it was able to exert crushing blows against Palestinians. In the War of Independence, Arab forces were overwhelmed and hundreds of thousands of Palestinians were displaced from their homes. More recently, Palestinians have been crowded into Gaza in ghastly living conditions. In the Occupied Territories Arabs live in appalling circumstances, hemmed in by innumerable restrictions and cut off from one another by an electrified security fence. Life in refugee camps elsewhere is similarly intolerable.

Israelis contend that this situation is ultimately the result of the intractability of Arabs who have never accepted a Jewish state in their midst. But leaving aside the question of who is right in this conflict, my point is that until recent times we Jews have never been in a position to protect Jewish interests through military power. Instead we have been victims. It has been our unfortunate role to be subject to the will of those who have despised and hated us.

Now that we have a country of our own, we too – like Christians and Muslims before us – can cause suffering and destruction. The powerless are now empowered. In one sense this is the tragedy of modern Jewish life. Yet, the Jewish community is united in its resolve never to endure the victimisation of the past. We are haunted by memories of the death camps where millions of Jews were led like lambs to the slaughter. We are determined that this shall not happen again. Across the Jewish world we insist that Hitler shall not have a posthumous victory.

George   Jews are sometimes accused of 'invoking the Holocaust' – appealing to the Holocaust to portray themselves as helpless victims. I fear this is what Dan is doing. He says that Judaism 'has until recent times not been in a position to conquer populations through armed conflict'. This is simply untrue. I have mentioned the Jewish invasion of Jericho where every Canaanite was massacred (Joshua 6:21), King Saul's annihilation of the Amalekites (1 Samuel 15:7–9), and the Jewish High Priest's instruction to Saul of Tarsus to take captive every Christian that he found (Acts 9:2). Certainly, these incidents are not within living memory, but then again neither is the Holocaust – although this is not to minimise Jewish suffering or in any way to condone Hitler's actions. Dan says that he is 'haunted by memories of the death camps': however, this is not a personal memory, but a reflection on modern Jewish history. Because the Jews succeeded in thoroughly annihilating the Canaanites and the Amalekites, they are no longer around to plead victim status, but of course the Jewish population can still invoke past atrocities.

The truth of the matter is that when a religious community is small and weak, it is easy prey for its opponents. The first century Christians were peaceable, because they were a persecuted minority. Who could fight back when thrown to lions in the Colosseum, or who could oppose the mighty Roman forces before Constantine allied himself with the Christians? Even so, despite being the largest religion in the world, Christians are arguably the most persecuted of all faiths. Pope Benedict XVI reckoned that they were the most persecuted of all religious believers, and the International Society for Human Rights has estimated that 80% of all acts of discrimination are against Christians. I would not like to press the statistical estimate, but certainly when one reflects on Christian history, one can identify serious persecution, not only under the Roman Empire, but also in the former Soviet Union, in North Korea, and in many parts of the Muslim world. True, there is no single example of six million members of our faith being eliminated in one single historical event, but over the centuries Christians have had more than their share of victimisation. But I don't think there's anything to be gained by Christians claiming victim status, as Dan wants to do on behalf of Jews.

There is another related issue on which I would like to comment. We have been discussing the extent to which religion causes violence, so we should distinguish between Jews as a religious group and as an ethnic one. The conflict between Arab and Jew in the Middle East is not predominantly an interreligious conflict. As I have argued previously, most conflicts are not about religion but about resources, land and ideology. In the case of Israel, nearly half of the Jewish population (somewhere between 42% and 46%, according to different surveys) identify themselves as secular. Hitler did not exterminate Jews on the grounds of their religion but because of spurious pseudo-scientific evidence relating to evolutionary theory. It was their ancestry, not their religion, that determined their fate during the Third Reich.

I think we can draw two conclusions from my argument. One is that religion is not the driving force in armed conflict, but rather these other factors I have mentioned. The second is that, unfortunately, a persecuted minority is seldom in a position to fight back, but once the victim gains power, the tables are turned, and all three of our religions have taken advantage of superior might. In that respect, we are all equally guilty.

CHAPTER 7

Do our traditions glorify violence?

Dying for one's faith is frequently regarded as meritorious. We hold martyrs and war heroes in high regard. We watch parades by armed forces and commemorate past military achievements. Is it good to be reminded of the human lives that have been sacrificed for just causes, or might we inadvertently be commending violence?

Dan In the Jewish tradition, martyrdom is referred to as 'Kiddush Ha-Shem' ('Sanctification of the Divine Name'). The Mishnah (*Berakhot* 9:5) interprets the commandment to love God with all thy soul (Deuteronomy 6:5) to mean with all thy life, that is to love him even at the cost of one's life. Against this, the verse from Leviticus 18:5, 'by the pursuit of which man shall live', is understood to mean live and not die, implying that martyrdom is not demanded in pursuit of the precepts of the Torah except in the case of idolatry, forbidden sexual relations and murder. The 12th century philosopher Moses Maimonides in *Yesodey Ha-Torah* 5:1–9 rules that a Jew may transgress the precepts of the Torah in order to save his life. But this does not apply to the above three offences, nor does it apply where the intention of heathens is to compel a Jew to commit an offence in order to demonstrate his disloyalty to the Jewish religion. Similarly, where there is a government decree against Jewish observance, a Jew is obliged to suffer martyrdom rather than transgress a minor precept even in private. Where martyrdom is not demanded, it is forbidden for a Jew to suffer martyrdom, and if he does, this is regarded as an act of suicide.

Jewish history records numerous examples of Jewish martyrdom in which martyrs offered up their lives regardless of whether the law required them to do so. Conversely, there were cases where the law required Jews to martyr themselves, but they failed to live up to the tradition. In the Middle Ages there are numerous examples of Jews being killed for professing their faith, and thereby dying as martyrs. Regarding those who died in the Holocaust, they are viewed as martyrs and are known as *kedoshim* (holy ones).

When faced with the destruction of Jewish communities by Muslim rulers, Maimonides gave the ruling that since Islam is not an idolatrous religion, martyrdom is not required if Jews are faced with the option of conversion or death. Other authorities, however, took issue, and argued that conversion to Islam involves a denial of the Torah of Moses and martyrdom is therefore demanded. With regard to Christianity, the rabbis ruled that martyrdom should be avoided by fleeing to places where it ceased to be a threat. This led to a tolerant attitude according to which those who had been forcibly converted to Christianity should be treated as unwitting offenders and welcomed back into the fold.

Although there were some sages such as Akiva who longed for martyrdom, in general Jews accepted martyrdom if necessary. Typical was the prayer of Isaiah Horowitz:

> O Holy God! If it be Thy will to bring me to this test, sanctify me and purify me and put into my thoughts and my mouth [the strength] to sanctify Thy name in public, as did the ten holy martyrs and myriads and thousands of Israel's saints . . . Our sages have taught us that whoever offers himself as a martyr for the sake of the sanctification of Thy name feels nothing of the great pain inflicted upon him. (Cited in Jacobs, 1995:337)

George When the Twin Towers were destroyed in the 9/11 attacks, President George W. Bush described the perpetrators as 'cowardly'. Despite the event being a terrible atrocity, the hijackers were certainly not cowards. To deliberately crash a plane, or to go into a crowded bus with explosives strapped around one's waist, knowing that one will not come out alive is a terrible thought for most of us, and something I would not care to contemplate, however just I thought my cause was.

Christians have typically commended martyrs who are prepared to give up their lives for their faith, and in the Christian faith martyrs and saints are particularly identified as special. In the Christian traditions where prayers for the dead are encouraged, saints and martyrs are excluded since their eternal life is assured. Their trophies and relics are venerated, and chapels and crypts are sometimes named in their honour. In his *City of God* (XXII:19) when discussing the resurrection, Saint Augustine stated that, while everyone else would receive a fully restored resurrection body, martyrs would still retain some of their wounds, since the marks of their ordeals would remain an integral part of their spiritual identity. Whether Christians today would take such a literal and physical view of the resurrection is doubtful, but Augustine's notion serves to highlight the esteem in which martyrs are held. The post-resurrection Jesus is invariably portrayed as retaining the wounds inflicted on his hands, feet and side during his passion, since Christ's atoning work cannot be separated from his self-sacrifice on the cross.

The martyr, however, differs significantly from the suicide bomber. Traditionally, the Church has viewed suicide as reprehensible, and until very recently suicides were denied burial in church grounds. The Church has taught that our lives are not our own but are lent to us by God, and the biblical teaching that we should love our neighbours as ourselves implies the need for self-love. (It should be said, however, that in recent times Christian leaders have been more sympathetic to suicide, acknowledging that some people can be so seriously distressed that they feel unable to continue with life.)

Christians would also be strongly opposed to taking the lives of innocent victims – or even enemies – as suicide terrorists do. The taking of innocent life is a clear violation of the fifth commandment, 'You shall not murder' (Exodus 20:13), and there are few biblical examples of God's people taking the lives of innocent parties for the sake of their faith. One interesting example in the Bible, however, is Samson. Having been blinded and bound in shackles by the Philistines, he rips down the pillars of their temple at a large religious festival, killing the entire congregation (Judges 16:23–31).

I imagine that this incident is as much an embarrassment for Dan as it is for me, since we share the same scriptures. Jesus' teaching is that one should refrain from retribution, and that those who are persecuted for their faith will inherit the kingdom of heaven (Matthew 5:10). It is popularly supposed that Muslims are more approving of suicide bombers, holding that those who die for their faith go directly to Paradise. I know this is far from the case, but I look forward to Dawoud's clarification.

Dawoud   In Islam, the act of martyrdom is known as *istishhad* and the martyr is a *shahid*. The earliest martyrs were those who, during the lifetime of the Prophet and the period of the Revelation, died for their refusal to abandon Islam or in the earliest battles against Quraysh, the pre-eminent Meccan tribe, who fiercely opposed the establishment of the new religion.

Martyrdom in Islam is closely linked with the notion of *jihad*, the struggle in the way of God. The Qur'an says:

> Those who leave their homes in the cause of Allah, and are then slain or die – On them will Allah bestow verily a goodly Provision: Truly Allah is He Who bestows the best provision. (22 Al-Hajj:58)

The Qur'an is clear: those who lay down their lives for their faith will enter Paradise immediately and will enjoy the rewards so graphically described. Their deaths are cause for celebration, not mourning:

> Think not of those who are slain in Allah's way as dead. Nay, they live, finding their sustenance in the presence of their Lord; they rejoice in the bounty provided by Allah. And with regard to those left behind, who have not yet joined them (in their bliss), the (Martyrs) glory in the fact that on them is no fear, nor have they (cause to) grieve. (3 Al Imran:169–170)

It is the current expression of this in so-called suicide missions that has been one of the highest profile and most alarming phenomena in the rise of Islamism over the last few decades. Despite the fact that suicide is forbidden in Islamic Law, in contemporary Muslim culture the word martyr has come to mean something closer to 'hero' rather than 'victim' – one who goes out actively to seek death by their own hand rather than simply one who accepts it at the hands of others because they cannot compromise their beliefs (although the latter would also earn the title of martyr). To most people, including most Muslims, the concept of strapping explosives to one's body and detonating them on a bus or in a restaurant is appalling. Yet we have become accustomed to seeing videos of sincere and obviously committed aspiring martyrs, mostly young and mostly male, expressing their deeply held belief that what they intend to do is God's will and will earn them eternal reward in Paradise.

George refers to the perpetrators of the attacks on the World Trade Center and the Pentagon in September 2001, challenging, irrespective of the horrific nature of these attacks, the assertion that they were cowards. He is, of course, right that no person in their right mind could embark upon something like this without fear or hesitation, yet the effect of the notion of martyrdom with which they have been indoctrinated is that they are not only unafraid of death but positively welcome it. It would be easy to suggest that these were the acts of desperate people with no hope for a future, but the 11 September attackers were mostly young professionals with careers and futures ahead of them. How can we even begin to counter such a threat which knows no fear and no deterrent and with which we cannot reason?

Dan   Dawoud has stated that most Muslims are shocked by suicide bombers; he states that the concept of strapping explosives on one's body and detonating them is appalling. Yet there is no doubt that in the Islamic world, there are vast numbers of Muslims who support such actions, believing that violent jihad is justified martyrdom rather than suicide. As Dawoud explains, the term 'suicide bombing' is actually a misnomer – a more accurate term is *shahid* (an act of martyrdom). The aim of the bomber is not suicide: the intention is to kill infidels in battle. Such an act is not simply permitted by Muhammad, but encouraged with promises of earthly reward in heaven. As the Qur'an states:

> Let those fight in the way of Allah who sell the liege of this world for the other. Whoso fighteth in the way of Allah, be he slain or be he victorious, on him We shall bestow a vast reward. (4:74)

This is the background to the numerous suicide bombings that have taken place in recent years. Such acts are promoted by an ideology that fosters martyrdom by promising Paradise to those who lose their lives in this way. Suicide bombing is thus an act of homicide. When Muslim apologists in the West argue that Islam is against suicide bombings by pointing to *hadith* that oppose killing oneself, they are being disingenuous. Muslims in the Arab world celebrate and revere suicide bombers, knowing that martyrdom in battle is glorified by their faith.

The mainstream OnIslam.net 2014 fatwa, for example, states that suicide operations are actually an obligatory form of jihad that has nothing to do with terrorism or suicide. In support of this claim, they quote Sheikh Faysal Mawlawi, deputy chairman of the European Council for Fatwa and Research, who argues that suicide bombings are 'a sacred duty carried out in form of self-defence in resisting aggression and injustice. So whoever is killed in such missions is a martyr, may Allah bless him with high esteem' (theReligionofPeace.com).

We in the West are thus faced with a serious dilemma. Both Jews and Christians seek to live in harmony with our Islamic neighbours. We regard ourselves as bound together in an Abrahamic umma. Yet, the spectre of militant jihad poses serious problems for mutual understanding. Moderate Muslims wish to distance themselves from such violent acts, claiming that violent jihad is not consonant with Islamic values. A number of Muslim scholars argue that suicide bombing is a clear violation of Islamic law and have characterised such acts against civilians as murderous and sinful. The Muslim scholar Muhammad Tahir-ul-Qadri targeted the rationale of Islamists by stating: 'Violence has no place in Islamic teaching, and no justification can be provided to it . . . good intention cannot justify a wrong and forbidden act' (https: en.m.wikipedia.org/wiki/Suicide_attack). In January 2006, one of Shi'i Islam's highest ranking Marja clerics, Ayatollah al-Udhma Yousof al-Sanei, decreed a fatwa against suicide bombing, declaring it a terrorist attack. Yet, despite such criticism of suicide bombing from within the Islamic world, there is no doubt that suicide attacks are carried out by devout Muslims who believe they are fulfilling Allah's will. Violent jihad is not an aberration of Islam but a central feature of Islamic life.

George   Christianity enables us to make a distinction between the martyr, the hero and the suicide. Martyrs die for their faith rather than any human cause, having been presented – usually by civil authorities – with a choice between apostasy or death. They do not fight back, but merely refuse to cooperate with those who attempt to force them to renounce their faith. Martyrs do not actively seek death, offering only passive resistance, and their acts of bravery consist solely in their willingness to die.

By contrast, heroes actively do brave deeds, sometimes at the cost of their own lives. Although there can be religious heroes, the hero's cause is generally a secular one. The hero may be responsible for an individual act of bravery, for example the firefighter who enters a burning building to rescue someone. However, we tend to honour collective groups of heroes, and mostly those who have risked or given their lives in armed combat. Any rewards are material or honorific: medals, ribbons, certificates of bravery, inscriptions on cenotaphs, and so on. British readers will of course be familiar the country's honours system, with its OBEs, CBEs and knighthoods.

The suicide typically differs both from the martyr and the hero. Suicides seek to solve life's problems by opting out rather than by passive resistance or brave perseverance. On rare occasions, military personnel have embarked on suicide missions to help win a war, but suicide is generally a means of escape. Whether it is an act of bravery or of cowardice is debatable; some courage must be involved in facing the unknown state of death and possible oblivion.

The division between church and state, which we typically find in the USA, Europe and elsewhere, enables Christians to ensure that martyrs are venerated in a religious context, while heroes are honoured by the state. Islam differs in acknowledging no separation between religion and politics, and hence it is difficult to establish the degree to which actions are religiously or politically motivated. Since ISIS aims to turn Iraq into an Islamic state with Shari'a law, there can be no distinction between political and religious objectives. However, as Dawoud has pointed out, since the majority of Muslims do not support such terrorist organisations, to suggest that that ISIS is part of Islam is rather like suggesting that the Ku Klux Klan is part of Christianity, and that Christians must share responsibility for its racist and violent policies.

Having said that Christianity enables the distinction between church and state, it should be acknowledged that state heroes are at times brought into a religious context, for example on Remembrance Sunday in the UK, or at celebrations to mark military anniversaries, such as V-J Day. I have to confess that I have mixed feelings on such occasions.

Certainly those who took part in the world wars made great sacrifices without which our lives might be very different – although subsequent wars like the Vietnam War, the Falklands War and the Iraq wars are more controversial. No doubt many Christians would disagree, but I would personally like to see less of the military parades on such occasions, and more reflection on how peace and reconciliation between warring parties might be attained. As John Milton wrote, 'Peace hath her victories no less renowned than war'. Perhaps the Churches could find more occasions on which to celebrate the victories of peace as well as those of war.

Dawoud   Dan's views on the nature of the threat of suicide bombings are understandable; this is a phenomenon of our age and the idea of a limitless supply of fanatics with no fear of death is indeed terrifying. The concept of suicide bombing is something that has only appeared in recent decades and was unheard of before around 1980. Promoted as a cult by the Iranian revolutionary regime, it took hold amongst the Palestinian resistance and spread from there through the conflict zones of the Middle East and beyond. I think, however, that the notion that the whole of the Muslim world is behind this kind of activity and rooting for the terrorists is something that parts of the media would like us to believe (and we will no doubt go on to discuss this in due course). When did we ever see a headline that read 'Hundreds of millions of Muslims worldwide sent their children to school and went to work today'? The media do not remind us so often that, for instance, thousands of Muslim doctors and nurses work in our hospitals and communities alongside their colleagues of all faiths and none, treating patients and saving lives without distinction as to faith or culture.

I do believe that Dan is wrong to think that all or most Muslims support such indiscriminate murderous acts, but it is of course easy to find all kinds of selective opinion and propaganda online supporting all kinds of ideas that are neither sound nor representative of the people they address. This does not make the incidents that do take place any less horrific, however, and he is not wrong to say that for those who do carry out such attacks, they are an act of absolute faith. For most of us it is almost impossible to comprehend, in part because we cannot grasp how an individual would take this ultimate step and throw away his or her life for no meaningful strategic or humanitarian benefit. We can understand altruism and the notion that people would risk their lives to save others, as we see in both military and civilian contexts, and we can understand how soldiers fighting for a cause might risk death in a military operation, but as George has discussed, such heroic deeds are not acts of faith but of morality, and no religion has the monopoly on this. From this point of view, so-called martyrdom missions might be considered an ultimate act of selfishness and self-absorption as the perpetrators act in the hope of reward, not believing that they are facing oblivion but that their place in Paradise is guaranteed, and with no tangible benefit to any other person but themselves.

What we might also point out is that many more Muslims than non-Muslims have been killed or maimed by suicide terror. However, whether we call it martyrdom or suicide terrorism, it is only a relatively small part of the turmoil that is going on in so many parts of the Muslim world, and the scale of the casualties that it has caused pales in comparison with the number of ordinary civilians obliterated by high tech weaponry, drones that kill by remote control and air strikes by foreign powers. To draw a moral distinction between these seems bizarre.

CHAPTER 8

Do all faiths persecute each other?

Violent conflicts often have a long history. Those who win by using physical force may be regarded as the victors, but such successes breed resentments and feelings of injustice which may surface when the opportunity arises. In this chapter we consider the past baggage that each of our three faiths brings to today's conflicts, and whether all three religions might be equally guilty of persecution and violence towards each other.

George Having co-authored with Dan and Dawoud on previous occasions, I have a fair idea of what Dan is likely to say on this theme. As a Jew, he will no doubt want to catalogue what has sometimes been called 'the longest hatred'. Gregory of Nyasa (331–396) described the Jews as 'slayers of the Lord, murderers of the prophets . . . advocates of the Devil', among other insults. Saint John Chrysostom – whose name means 'gold mouth' and whom Christians commended for his excellent preaching – accused them of sacrificing their children to Satan, describing the synagogue as 'a brothel, a den of scoundrels, the temple of demons devoted to idolatrous cults . . . a place of meeting for the assassins of Christ'. He described the Jews as having 'fallen into a condition lower than the vilest animal. Debauchery and drunkenness have brought them to the level of the lusty goat and the pig'. (The last remark, of course, is particularly insulting, since Jews regard the pig as an unclean animal.) Augustine accused them of being 'wilfully blind to Holy Scripture', and Martin Luther recommended that their synagogues should be set on fire, their houses razed, their wealth and their copies of the Talmud confiscated, and that they should be denied safe passage on the highways.

Sadly, this is only a small sample of antisemitic statements by Christians. Historically, the principal historical objection to Jews is that they rejected Jesus as the Messiah. When Pontius Pilate asked the Jewish crowd whether Jesus should be crucified, they replied, 'His blood is on us and on our children!' (Matthew 27:25), and this response has been taken to be Jewish acceptance of communal intergenerational guilt for Jesus' death, and has been used to justify their persecution throughout the ages.

If we turn to Islam, Christians have done their share of persecuting too, most notably in the Crusades, when the Christian armies on entering Jerusalem indiscriminately slaughtered Jews and Muslims. Christians have always disliked the suggestion that there might be a new prophet superseding Jesus or new scriptures beyond the Old and New Testaments. Islam, of course, has both, and the concept of *jihad*, reinforced by terrorist attacks, has done little to allay prejudice. Happily, the Christian faith allows for repentance, forgiveness, and for progress. One of the outcomes of the Second Vatican Council was Pope Paul VI's declaration *Nostra Aetate*, which stated that 'what happened in [Christ's] passion cannot be charged against all the Jews, without distinction, then alive, nor against the Jews of today', and which outlaws persecution in general. This judgement would find acceptance not merely with Catholics, but by the majority of present-day Christians.

However, we could equally cite examples of considerable persecution against Christians. In a previous contribution I mentioned the claim that Christians can claim to be the most persecuted of all faiths, particularly in Islamic countries. One web site lists the worst offenders, after North Korea, as Somalia, Iraq, Syria, Afghanistan, Sudan, Iran and Pakistan (Open Doors, 2015).

There is a risk that this section of our discussion could turn into a catalogue or a competition to determine which faith has inflicted or endured the most suffering. My challenge to Dawoud and Dan – and also to myself – is to ask how we can take this discussion constructively forward. What can we do about our past? How can we overcome the legacy of past hatred and persecution? Is there any way in which our three faiths can show forgiveness and reconciliation?

Dawoud As George says, we could fill pages simply cataloguing acts of persecution between faiths. Since the earliest times, peoples have persecuted each other on grounds of faith, ethnicity, origin or some permutation of these elements and others.

If we want to explore how we can resolve or come to terms with some of the grievances that have blighted the lives of so many generations both ancient and modern, I think we have to look at why peoples persecute each other. How do we define persecution as distinct from a balance of hostilities between groups of different identities? If we take an overview of the history of persecution, there appear to be common elements, of which the most fundamental is the balance of power, but why do the powerful feel the need to oppress, torment or destroy the weak? I think the most basic answer is, because they can. By cultivating a sense of the 'otherness' of the weak, those with power can rally their own communities and consolidate the sense of their own identity as contrasted with their victims who are deemed weak and deserving of contempt, or who may be portrayed as a threat to the integrity of a community that may undermine it from within, either morally or materially, and who must therefore be controlled or destroyed.

During the very early years of Islam in Mecca, the first Muslims were persecuted by Quraysh as the promotion of monotheism threatened to undermine the foundations of the city and its livelihood that was based on worship of the idols in the Ka'aba. There are numerous accounts of persecution ranging from verbal abuse to physical attacks and acts of torture intended to pressurise people into recanting their beliefs. It has been suggested that it was this persecution that turned what was a peaceful mission to bring people to faith in one god into a more militant movement of conversion and expansion. The parts of the Qur'an revealed at Mecca in the early years are mostly concerned with faith and reward in the hereafter, whereas those revealed in Medina after the flight from Meccan persecution are more to do with organisation, including mobilisation against those who threaten the Muslim community.

Episodes of persecution appear across time and are not limited to the relationships between our three faiths in broad terms, but also to treatment of those of other faiths and the sectarian divisions within our own faiths. Historically, both Islam and Christianity in the form of missionary activity and empire building have been guilty of abuses of other cultures, culminating in one of the greatest crimes against humanity, the slave trade, in which both Christians and Muslim slave traders were complicit. In the present, we are seeing unspeakable atrocities committed by the so-called Islamic State both against non-Muslims, including the Yazidis and Christians, and against Shi'i Muslims.

George has pointed out the element of dehumanising language which is common to most cases of persecution. I believe that it is absolutely essential that we are vigilant against this in our own safe world where it is becoming increasingly common, for example, to find references to refugees and migrants in the tabloid press and even by senior politicians in terms that undermine their humanity and turn them into 'the other', thereby justifying at worst their mistreatment by the authorities and at best our ignoring of their plight.

Dan   George has correctly anticipated that I would want to catalogue the history of Jewish persecution. He is right, but I want to stress that the suffering that Jews have endured at the hands of Christians is different from our treatment by Muslims. Judaism is the oldest of our three faiths. For nearly 4,000 years we have been a minority people. Until the present day, it has never been possible for Jews to persecute Muslims or Christians. Rather we have been the persecuted. Under Islam, Jews were regarded as second-class citizens as were Christians, but they were never subjected to the same intolerance and hatred as Jews experienced in Christian lands.

In the Graeco-Roman world, Jews were regarded with contempt. With the emergence of Christianity such hostility intensified. The New Testament served as the basis for the early Church's vilification of the Jews. According to the Church Fathers, the Jewish people are lawless and dissolute. Because of their rejection of Christ, the Jewish nation has been excluded from God's grace and is subject to his wrath.

This *Adversus Judaeos* teaching of the early Church Fathers continued into the medieval period. During the Crusades, Christian mobs massacred Jewish communities. Jews were charged with killing Christian children to use their blood for ritual purposes, with blaspheming Christ and Christianity in their sacred texts, and with causing the Black Death by poisoning wells. Throughout the Middle Ages Jews were detested, and the image of the satanic Jew became a central feature of Western iconography. Repeatedly Jews were accused of satanic activities and viewed as a sub-species of the human race.

In the post-medieval period such negative stereotypes of the Jews became a central feature of Eastern and Western European culture. In Germany the rise of a sense of national identity and self-confidence fuelled antisemitic feelings. Such Judeophobia served as the background to the rise of Nazism, and as hostility towards Jewry intensified, Church leaders acquiesced in the onslaught against the Jewish population.

This history of hostility towards Jewry has been largely a Christian phenomenon. However, with the establishment of a Jewish homeland in Palestine, Arab nations have united against Israel and this has led to the rise of antagonism towards Jews in general. Typical of modern diatribes against the Jewish community is a 1974 tract, *Holy War and Victory*, written by Abdel-Halim Mahmoud, the former Rector of Cairo's Al-Azhar University. In his view, the struggle for Islam is depicted as a struggle against Satan:

> Among Satan's friends – indeed his best friends in our age – are the Jews. They have laid down a plan for undermining humanity, religiously and ethically. They have begun their work to implement this plan with their money and the propaganda. They have falsified knowledge, exploited the pens of writers and bought minds in their quest for the ruination of humanity. (Mahmoud; in Cohn-Sherbok, 2002:342)

Such a denunciation parallels medieval Christian polemics against the Jews. As a result of such perceptions, many fundamentalist Muslims today are intent on carrying out a jihad against the Jewish community. As one of humanity's most persistent hatreds, antisemitism thus continues to flourish in the modern world. Nearly forty centuries of antipathy towards Jews has not diminished despite the determination of the Jewish people to free itself from the scourge of prejudice and misunderstanding. Even though the Jewish people are now empowered in their own country, Jewish security is as imperilled as it was in previous centuries. Yet I believe that Jews, Christians and Muslims can take steps towards greater sympathy and understanding – this book itself is an example of what can be done.

George Dawoud identifies the balance of power and a perception of otherness as factors giving rise to persecution. Another important factor is solidarity. Persecuted minorities tend to make themselves readily identifiable as cohesive groups. They often share similar cultural traits, for example skin colour or physique, and they have a group identity, typically marrying within their own communities, sometimes wearing distinctive dress, and living together in definable geographical areas, which are sometimes pejoratively referred to as ghettos. They have their own customs and festivals: in the case of Jews the observance of the Sabbath and Passover, and for Muslims the observance of Ramadan.

Such differences are often erroneously perceived as threats by the dominant culture, whose more reactionary members dislike apparent challenges to their lifestyle or to their religion. As a result, they can inflict a range of sanctions against such minorities, ranging from subjection to ridicule and misrepresentation to more serious abuse such as denial of access to education and employment, restrictions on freedom, torture, rape, abduction and even death.

By continuing to list the examples of persecution against Jews, Dan reminds us of one important feature of persecution – its ineffectiveness. It is very rare for a religious community to be wiped out through persecution: the Cathars of 14th century France are the exception rather than the rule. Persecution usually serves to reinforce a determination to practise one's faith and not give in. Despite the 'longest hatred', the Jews continue to exist, while the Nazi persecutors have died out.

The persecuted minority, paradoxically, therefore holds some measure of power over their opponents who feel threatened by them. They must be doing or teaching something important if the authorities want to put them down. This is no doubt why Jesus regarded persecution as something commendable and positive. Jesus said, 'Blessed are those who are persecuted because of righteousness, for theirs is the kingdom of heaven' (Matthew 5:10). Jesus was offering more than reassurance that victims of persecution would be rewarded for their perseverance: steadfastness and endurance are marks of belonging to God's kingdom. The early Church Father Tertullian (160–220) wrote, 'The blood of martyrs is the seed of the Church' (*Apology*:50). Persecution and martyrdom give rise to determination, and the Christians might simply have died out as a minor

Jewish sect if their detractors had chosen to ignore them. The Christian response has been to accept persecution, and indeed to welcome it. Paul wrote, 'When we are cursed, we bless; when we are persecuted, we endure it; when we are slandered, we answer kindly' (1 Corinthians 4:12–13).

Jesus' words on the cross included a prayer for his persecutors: 'Father, forgive them, for they do not know what they are doing' (Luke 23:34). This highlights the fact that persecutors are frequently unaware of the implications of their actions. No doubt Christians have been unaware of the rightful place of Jews in the world, just as the 1st century Jews did not realise that they could not obliterate the emergent Christians. Those Muslims who have persecuted the Baha'i are also unaware that this faith presents no serious threat to Islam, and that their actions have only caused the Baha'i to spread worldwide as they have been forced to flee from Iran. Ending persecution and forgiving past persecution are therefore two important goals, towards which we all need to strive.

Dawoud   I am sure that none of us would want to dispute or underestimate the scale of the persecution of Jews over the centuries, particularly in the Christian West. In the light of the Jewish experience in the 20th century, Dan is perfectly justified in focusing on this pattern of abuse. Jews, however, like Muslims and Christians, are not themselves a single homogeneous community.

Within all of our faiths there are factions and divisions which are equally open to discrimination, persecution and outright hostility. Muslim majorities, both Sunna and Shi'a, have persecuted each other where they exist as minorities within their populations and, as George has described, maintain their beliefs, identities and traditions, and are prepared to die (and sometimes to kill) for them. Within each of these there are many smaller groups, such as the Ahmadiyya, who are considered to be a heretical sect by both Shi'a and Sunna, and who are subject to extreme discrimination and persecution.

In addition, there are ethnic divisions that are equally insurmountable. While claiming religious brotherhood in grand rhetorical terms, many Muslims would not allow their children to marry another Muslim of a different ethnicity. We only have to look at the migrant worker communities in the wealthy Arab countries who have provided the manual labour to build the shining cities of the Gulf States and who drive the cars and clean the houses of the well-off to see how people are prepared to subject fellow Muslims, fellow human beings, to working conditions and standards of living that they would find unacceptable for themselves, effectively deeming their lives to be of less value than their own – just as some privileged Christians in the United States are prepared to exploit other Christian migrant workers to do some of the things that they are not prepared to do themselves for rates of pay that they would not consider acceptable.

During the early waves of immigration to the State of Israel, Middle Eastern Jews were subject to discrimination by their Western co-religionists and forced to conform to a Western cultural model. They were pressured to abandon their traditional dress, which had made them almost indistinguishable from the Arab communities amongst whom they had lived for centuries, and discouraged from speaking their native Arabic or listening to their traditional music. They tended to take up the more menial jobs and to live in the poorer areas. While considerable assimilation has taken place, there is still a gap in expectations and aspirations and the Middle Eastern Jews are still regarded by many as culturally inferior. In addition, there are Orthodox communities who, while enjoying the privileges of living within the protection of the Jewish state, maintain a degree of separation from the rest of the population.

George stresses that ending persecution and moving forward from past persecution should be our goals and, as Dan points out, promoting greater understanding and empathy is what we are trying achieve here. As we have mentioned in previous discussions, in terms of worldview the three of us perhaps have more in common with each other than we do with many of our fellow Muslims, Christians and Jews. We are able to separate our personal relationship with our God from our social and political outlook, or perhaps it is our own interpretation of our faith that underpins our social and political outlook, and in this we are in a sense speaking to a self-selecting audience. For much of the world this is not the case, but this does not mean that we should not continue to contribute to the dialogue.

Dan George has pointed out that there is a paradoxical aspect to persecution: even though it is inherently evil, persecution can actually strengthen the faithful. Several years ago I wrote a book along these lines entitled *The Paradox of Anti-Semitism* (2006). In this study I stressed that through our long history we Jews have been subjected to suffering and murder. Yet, it is precisely such antipathy which has driven us together and ensured that we remain faithful to the Jewish heritage.

For centuries Jews lived isolated lives, set apart from the societies in which they resided. As a minority group we were viewed as aliens. In *The Jewish State*, Theodor Herzl, the father of modern Zionism, decried such discrimination and argued that we Jews will never be secure unless we have a state of our own. This perception has been the driving force of the Jewish determination to establish a homeland in Palestine. Since the Enlightenment in the late 17th century, the Jewish people have sought to free themselves from the fetters of persecution. The creation of Israel coupled with assimilation and integration in other countries have been the two central means whereby we have struggled to escape from centuries of hatred.

In large part we have been successful. No longer are we a vulnerable people, stateless and alien. Instead we have embraced modernity and have shed the disabilities of the past. Yet in doing so, the Jewish heritage which bound us to one another and provided a sense of stability in a world where we were detested has disintegrated. In contemporary society – in Israel as well as in other lands – Jews have largely detached themselves from the ancient traditions which served as the lifeblood of Jewish existence. Jew-hatred has largely disappeared except in Arab lands. But in this process traditional Jewish beliefs and practices have been lost.

No one wishes to return to a ghetto-like existence. However, we should recognise that persecution of the Jew – which has been a hallmark of Western society in the past – held us together in the face of centuries of hostility. It has been our destiny to be God's suffering servant, witnessing to God's revelation on Mount Sinai. Faithful to God's revealed word, we have been able to endure torture and death. In contemporary society all this has changed. In Western countries we are no longer despised. Instead we are being loved to death.

What is at stake is nothing less than the ancient beliefs and practices of the past. As I stressed, persecution is to be decried. It is a major evil. It needs to be condemned and resisted. But, at the same time, we should recognise the truth of what George has said. Persecution can strengthen the innocent. It can bind us together in defiance of the forces that seek to crush us. Jewish martyrs, like their Christian counterparts, went to their deaths assured of divine reward.

Today Jews living in Western counties are spared the agonies of past generations. We have broken free of the ghetto walls that confined us. Through assimilation and the establishment of our own homeland, we are no longer victims of misunderstanding and hatred. Our changed circumstances are to be celebrated. But such freedom comes at a cost.

CHAPTER 9

The role of the media

We rely largely on media reports about terror, violence and war, and their relationship to religion. How biased or unbiased are they? Do they sensationalise, encouraging prejudice? To what extent are they concerned to provide an accurate portrayal of events, or do they simply want to sell newspapers and attract advertisers?

Dawoud To what extent do the media foster violence and prejudice? We like to think that the media all around us are manipulative and sometimes even sinister, but in countries where there is freedom of information and expression, the media that each of us chooses reflect our attitudes and beliefs. This has always been the case with the mainstream traditional media and particularly newspapers. There has always been a general divide between the Left and the Right and whether we choose to read the *The Guardian* or the *Daily Mail*, *The Telegraph* or *The Sun*, we are for the most part self-selecting audiences whose outlooks are formed by our backgrounds and education. We read and listen to the things that make us feel secure, that tell us that what we think and feel is justified, and we ridicule and condemn those that are diametrically opposed to them. While the mainstream media rarely create our views, they do feed their messages to their target audiences, sustaining their worldviews and nurturing their prejudices, however sinister or benign, often with no more important purpose for their publishers than keeping their target groups captive in order to aim commercial marketing at them. Language and labels are and always have been key to this. A person may be a terrorist or a freedom fighter or martyr, a migrant or a refugee, and large groups of refugees or migrants may be a 'swarm' as recently described by the former British Prime Minister David Cameron, or the 'huddled masses yearning to breathe free' (from *The New Colossus* by Emma Lazarus, engraved on a plaque inside the Statue of Liberty).

Over the last two decades or so, however, there has been a revolution in the media. We are no longer restricted to a few audio, visual and print media sources. The social media generation is not a passive recipient of news and information. Today, everyone is the media. Events may be recorded on smartphones and sent around the world in seconds, news items and opinions are selected, shared and commented upon, whether openly or amongst groups, and communities and networks are formed. This may be a force for good or for ill. Independent journalists and film-makers can broadcast objective investigations or produce the vilest propaganda. Many of the younger generation no longer rely on mainstream news media but question everything. Every part of the media is subjected to scrutiny, comment and rebuttal. While social media may be used as a tool for propaganda, radicalisation and recruitment of jihadists, it was also a crucial element in the eruption and organisation of the so-called Arab Spring. Simple internet searches will bring up some of the nastiest antisemitic, anti-Western, Islamic fundamentalist, Islamophobic and racially bigoted material imaginable and yet at the same time show some of the most uplifting and humane responses to all kinds of prejudice and injustice. On balance I feel that free worldwide media are a force for good as the democratisation of information limits or at least monitors the control that the major media owners and governments can exert, and opens the debate to all.

Dan Dawoud is right: there now exist a wide range of media outlets covering the full spectrum of political opinions. In all cases media sources seek to gain as large an audience as possible. Regrettably, this means that sensationalist news inevitably occupies a central role in newspapers, magazines, radio and television. As a consequence, those who use terror to promote their political aims are constantly in the news. Terrorists are daily able to capture the headlines through acts of violence and destruction.

There is now considerable scholarly evidence that the reporting of violence can trigger further attack. Michael Jetter, a lecturer at the University of Western Australia in Perth, for example, analysed more than 60,000 terrorist attacks between 1970 and 2012 as reported in *The New York Times*. In his view, terrorism causes media attention and vice versa, leading to an inflationary spiral.

Terrorist groups have also exploited the internet to spread their message and attract recruits. Al-Qaeda was the first to use the web extensively. Viewing itself as a global movement, it depended on a global communications network to reach its constituents. It sees its mission as not simply creating terror among its foes but awakening the Muslim community. Its leaders view communications as a central element in this struggle.

More recently ISIS uses the media to their advantage when releasing videos of beheadings and the destruction of ancient archaeological sites. Posting executions online gives ISIS the power to manipulate and cause havoc among the general population. In response, Western government officials have urged social media companies to stop hosting content from ISIS and other terror groups. However, there has been criticism from various quarters that such censorship undermines freedom of speech.

Today the internet serves as the single most important venue for the radicalisation of Islamic youth. By its very nature, the internet is ideal for such activity. Most notably it offers:

- easy access,

- little or no regulation, censorship or other forms of government control,

- potentially huge audiences spread throughout the world,

- anonymity of communication,

- fast flow of information,

- inexpensive development and maintenance of a web presence,

- a multimedia environment with the ability to combine text, graphics, audio and video,

- the promotion of films, songs, books and posters.

Yet, the use of violence is not restricted to the Islamic world. Groups and organisations which have taken advantage of the internet include:

Middle East: Hamas (the Islamic Resistance Movement), the Lebanese Hezbollah (Party of God), the Al-Aqsa Martyrs' Brigades, Fatah Tanzim, the Popular Front for the Liberation of Palestine (PFLP), the Palestinian Islamic Jihad, the Kahane Lives movement, the People's Mujahedin of Iran (PMOI), the Kurdish Workers' Party (PKK), the Turkish-based Popular Democratic Liberation Front Party (DHKP/C) and the Great East Islamic Raiders Front (IBDA-C).

Europe: the Basque ETA movement, Armata Corsa (the Corsican Army) and the Irish Republican Army (IRA).

Latin America: Peru's Túpac Amaru (MRTA) and Shining Path (Sendero Luminoso), the Colombian National Liberation Army (ELN-Colombia) and the Revolutionary Armed Forces of Colombia (FARC).

Asia: Al-Qaeda, the Japanese Supreme Truth (Aum Shinrikyo), Ansar al-Islam (Supporters of Islam) in Iraq, the Japanese Red Army (JRA), Hizb-ul Mujahideen in Kashmir, the Liberation Tigers of Tamil Eelam (LTTE), the Islamic Movement of Uzbekistan (IMU), the Moro Islamic Liberation Front (MILF) in the Philippines, the Pakistan based Lashkar-e-Taiba and the rebel movement in Chechnya (www.usip.org).

Terrorists now fight their wars in cyberspace as well as on the ground. This is the new battlefront.

George I have to agree with Dawoud and Dan's analysis of how the media provide sensationalist accounts of violence and terrorism to a self-selecting readership. Newspapers need to make a profit, and most readers prefer to read about events that confirm their own views rather than challenge their opinions. I am no exception, of course. When the editor of a church newsletter stated that he was 'white, British, Christian and proud of it', I requested him to send no further editions, since I have no wish to be converted to racial and religious prejudice. (Sadly, one cannot always rely on churches to promote tolerance.)

Journalists too have incentives to write sensationalist articles. Since they are paid more for front page copy, they are likely to exaggerate an account to make it look exciting, rather than provide a staid and balanced report. Reports of Abu Hamza at the Finsbury Park mosque in London were more likely to attract readers than accounts of Sufi dervishes dancing! The media can also create news rather than merely report it, and sometimes even fabricate stories. For example, a tabloid editor once asked a (male) journalist to dress up in a burqa for a day to report public reactions! (The value of such reportage was not explained.) One might think that having more Muslim journalists working in Western media might improve matters, but editors can have unrealistic or stereotypical expectations about Muslim journalists. It has been suggested – in all seriousness – to several Muslim journalists that they might try to infiltrate Al-Qaeda in the interests of writing interesting material (*The Guardian*, 19 November 2007).

Of course, we are all familiar with the media associating Islam with and concepts like *jihad* (usually misunderstood as 'holy war'), terrorism, violence and extremism, not to mention controversial practices such as female genital mutilation, *halal* (sometimes inappropriately called 'ritual slaughter' of animals) and the wearing of burqas. Even expressions like 'Islam and the West' tacitly suggest that Muslims are outsiders, when of course substantial numbers of Muslims now live in the West and enjoy good relations with other citizens in the workplace and in schools and colleges.

It is often argued that there are adequate safeguards against misrepresentation, notably libel laws, and the Press Complaints Commission (PCC) with its Code of Practice for editors and journalists. However, laws of libel offer little protection to religious communities. A *religion* cannot sue a newspaper, and if specific individuals or religious organisations are libelled, they are unlikely to want to risk the huge legal expenses that newspapers can readily afford. The PCC's Code of Practice states that '[t]he Press must take care not to publish inaccurate, misleading or distorted information', that prejudicial or pejorative reference to race, colour and religion (among other characteristics) must be avoided, and that any such details must be genuinely relevant to material that is published. However, these regulations are frequently unobserved and unenforced.

Dawoud mentions the internet, and I agree with him that it works for good and for ill. As far as religious communities are concerned, it offers the advantage of disseminating their beliefs and practices, unfiltered by journalists or opponents. On the other hand, it also enables organisations like Britain First to express its vehement opposition to mosque building. While social media allow freedom of speech to anyone who can access the World Wide Web, it is often quite depressing to see the amount of hatred and prejudice that is unleashed on Facebook pages or comments boxes underneath news items.

We can certainly access opinions more freely as information technology progresses, but I don't know whether this results in greater education and less prejudice.

Dawoud   The explosion in the production and availability of media and particularly those forms facilitated by the internet has changed our world and, while we may sometimes feel overwhelmed by the constant 'noise' that surrounds us, I am inclined to believe that overall it is a positive element in facilitating freedom of expression and freedom of information. Where once our news sources were limited, we now have access to the whole world, often in real time, and to a range of perspectives on every question, and we have the right and the ability to contribute our own. The media make us aware of issues that are important to all of us, allow us to question everything and to challenge those in power. They facilitate the exchange of information and opinion between people all over the world. We do not have to believe everything that we are told, and gradually around the world it is becoming increasingly difficult for repressive governments and regimes to control information, or for those in positions of power to cover up wrongdoing.

George is right about the creation of stereotypes in the media and the harmful effects that these may have. It has been suggested that an important element in the attitude of many people to the refugee crisis facing Europe at the time of writing is a long-standing prejudice that has been fostered by the media towards people of Asian, Middle Eastern and African origin in general and Muslims in particular. If those risking their lives to cross the Mediterranean fleeing from war and persecution were white, Christian or Jewish, would the media speak about them and treat them in the same way? If we were seeing British, Dutch or American families with children washed up on beaches or camping under plastic sheets in fields, would popular reaction be different? I have referred in previous discussions between us to a study by Jack Shaheen who has catalogued and analysed the way that the film industry has treated Arabs (generally referred to inseparably from Muslims) over a century. In his *Reel Bad Arabs: How Hollywood Vilifies a People,* he shows us stereotype portrayals of bandits, wealthy oil sheikhs, lechers, misogynists, villains and terrorists in some 900 films. He quotes the author Sam Keen who says: 'You can hit an Arab free; they're free enemies, free villains – where you couldn't do it to a Jew or you can't do it to a black anymore'. Such stereotypes permeate our unconscious thoughts and dictate our reactions to those whom we see as different to ourselves.

At the same time the plight of the refugees shown in the mainstream media and spread around the world on social media has produced a massive humanitarian reaction amongst people of all nationalities and religious communities all over Europe, and it is social media that have enabled these to mobilise to offer what help they can to those in need and to put pressure on their governments to respond to the crisis.

Dan Dawoud is right that the opening up of the internet has had a profoundly important positive impact. It has provided a simple means of access to a world of information. Never before has it been possible to obtain such a wealth of material. This has profoundly changed the nature of education at every level. In addition, the opportunity to download ebooks means that despite where one lives, it is now possible to obtain both old and new books in a matter of minutes. This is true as well of newspapers and magazines, as well as news websites. This is an unprecedented revolution. We are fortunate to live in such exciting times. Yet accompanying this explosion of information is the fact that the web is being used as a resource for those intent on causing violence and terror. We have touched on the ways in which the internet is employed by jihadists and others. This is the dark side of the World Wide Web that cannot be ignored.

I want to turn, however, to the issue of migration that is currently the focus of news attention. Here Dawoud and I part company. He maintains that the media has reinforced negative stereotypes of refugees now flooding into Europe. He writes that news sources foster prejudice against people of Asian, Middle Eastern and African origin in general and Muslims in particular. He asks: 'If those risking their lives to cross the Mediterranean fleeing from war and persecution were white,

Christian or Jewish, would the media speak about them and treat them in the same way?'

There are two points I would make about this argument. First, there has been an outpouring of sympathy for migrants who are suffering on this long journey to Europe. Images of drowned children have particularly evoked an overwhelming response. I do not believe that there is prejudice against Asians, Middle Eastern or Muslim migrants. Rather, many in the West have responded with heartfelt empathy for their plight. Yet – and this is my second observation – there is no doubt that there is a strong suspicion amongst Europeans that the majority of these migrants are not fleeing from war zones or evil regimes. Instead, they are economic migrants who seek to make a new life in prosperous European countries.

This would not be an aberration; rather in modern times it has been common for those living abject lives to settle in countries with economic advantages. Indeed, this was true of my grandparents who left Hungary for New York. For them the United States offered opportunities that were closed to them in Eastern Europe. Yet there is a fundamental contrast between Jews like my grandparents who left Europe for America and those seeking to escape into Europe. Jews who immigrated to America were compelled to go through official immigration procedures. Today migrants flooding across borders seek to enter Europe illegally. It is not surprising that political leaders as well as the general public are alarmed by the implications of such migration. If these new immigrants are to be absorbed into European countries, this will require a considerable financial outlay. It is not prejudice but a real concern about the ways Western economies and community infrastructures will be affected by this influx that has caused dismay and concern.

George   Dan says, 'I do not believe that there is prejudice against Asians, Middle Eastern or Muslim migrants'. I just spent five minutes perusing the comments boxes of a random *Mail Online* report about migrants and the Syrian crisis (http://www.dailymail.co.uk/news/article-3240010/ Number-refugees-arriving-Europe-soars-85-year-just-one-five-war-torn-Syria.html#comments). Quoting all the prejudiced comments would occupy far more space than I'm allocated here, but samples include:

- I hate the litter Theyre a bunch of conscript avoiders.

- send all the single men back to their countries of origin

- there are far too many flooding in

- ill be waiting at dover with there return tickets. whos with me?

- we let to many forigen people in

- Only a matter of time now, and the whole world will be m-us-lim

(Spelling and punctuation are all as in the original text. It is interesting that immigrants are sometimes criticised for lacking knowledge of English!)

True, there are contributors who write in support of the refugees, but it is worrying that there are so many comments along the lines of the above. While it is true that some immigrants are economic migrants, this is unlikely to be true of people who are prepared to live in shanty towns in Calais or travel for long periods on unsafe boats, with standing room only, prepared to risk their lives to escape from a war-torn country. It is telling that one seldom hears objections to immigrants from the USA, Canada or Australia, for example – which reinforces Dawoud's point that there is still a significant amount of racial and religious prejudice against settlers from the Middle East and Africa, most of whom are people of colour, or who are Muslim, Sikh or Hindu, rather than Christian or non-religious.

As both Dan and Dawoud have mentioned, the internet can be used for good or for harm. Those with access can not only read the news reports and discussions, but can join in the debate. On the one hand this allows the racists and Islamophobes to unleash their xenophobic prejudices, but it also enables those who are better informed to offer more balanced responses, and to circulate proper information about numbers of immigrants and their likely effect on an increasingly multicultural and multi-religious population, as we have in Britain.

Sometimes the level of online discussion is no more than the high-tech equivalent of a chat in a pub, but at other times social media can create genuine change. The story of a 3-year-old refugee boy whose body was washed up on a Turkish beach while his family were attempting to flee Syria to get to Greece, caused many people to think less about the available space in Britain, and more about the plight of the Syrians. Up to that point, many British citizens were demanding strict controls on immigration, insisting that Britain was full and that further immigrants (by which they tacitly meant immigrants from the Middle East and Asia) should be denied entry. The story of the dead infant, which was widely shared on social media, to some degree turned the tide of opinion, causing the public to focus on the refugees' predicament rather than available space in Britain.

The internet certainly allows all viewpoints to have an airing. However, since so many people now contribute to Facebook posts, blogs and comments, it becomes difficult to ensure that one's views are read by a reasonably wide audience.

CHAPTER 10

Religious identities

The media typically give a religious identity to 'Islamic' terrorist groups. Yet the Irish Republican Army is seldom, if ever, described as a Christian terrorist organisation. How justifiable is it to give some terrorists a religious identity? Should the media be more wary of associating violence with specific religions?

Dan As we noted previously, terrorism is not a new concept. Yet it is difficult to define. The term is applied to various violent actions. It can connote a justified reaction to oppression, a holy act, or a crime against humanity. In each case the understanding depends on the views of beholders and participants. In the United States, the Department of Defense defines terrorism as follows: 'The calculated use of unlawful violence or threat of unlawful violence to inculcate fear; intended to coerce or to intimidate governments or societies in the pursuit of goals that are generally political, religious or ideological'. Within this definition, there are three key elements – violence, fear and intimidation. The US Federal Bureau of Investigation (FBI) uses this definition: 'Terrorism is the unlawful use of force and violence against persons or property to intimidate or coerce a government, the civilian population, or any segment thereof, in furtherance of political or social objectives'. The US Department of State defines terrorism as 'premeditated politically-motivated violence perpetrated against non-combatant targets by sub-national groups or clandestine agents, usually intended to influence an audience' (International Security and Terrorism Research, 2016).

Outside the United States, there are greater variations in what features of terrorism are stressed. In 1974 the British government defined terrorism simply as 'the use of violence for political ends, and includes any use of violence for the purpose of putting the public or any section of the public, in fear'. The United Nations in 1992 defined terrorism as 'an anxiety-inspiring method of repeated violent action, employed by (semi-)clandestine individual, group, or state actors, for idiosyncratic, criminal or political reasons, whereby – in contrast to assassination – the direct targets of violence are not the main targets' (International Security and Terrorism Research, 2016).

Despite the range of such definitions, there is no doubt that the strategy of terrorists is to commit acts of violence which draw the attention of the local population, the government and the world to their cause. The effectiveness of such acts lies not in the act itself, but in the public's and government's reaction. Most recently, for example, beheadings carried out by ISIS were designed to strike fear into the millions of people who witnessed such acts. In assessing the impact of such actions, there are three perspectives that need to be considered: the terrorist's, the victim's and the general public's. From the terrorist's point of view, they are acting as brave champions of their cause. Victims and the general public, on the other hand, regard terrorist action as an evil danger that must be curtailed.

At present, militant Islamic terrorism – rooted in the Middle East and South Asia – has taken centre stage. Since 1989 the increasing willingness of religious extremists to strike at targets outside their immediate country or region underscores the global nature of such terrorist activity. The religious basis for such attacks must not be underestimated. Currently there is a tendency to dismiss the theological underpinning of Islamic acts of terrorism. This is a mistake. There is no doubt that Muslim suicide bombers who martyr themselves for the faith believe that they are acting for the greater glory of Allah, convinced that their actions will be rewarded in the hereafter. Such violent jihad is grounded in the conviction that an otherworldly power sanctions and commands such acts.

George   Dan insists that the religious basis of Islamic terrorist organisations should not be underestimated, and he has consistently contended that groups like ISIS are part of Islam. While it is true that ISIS, the Taliban, Al-Qaeda and Boko Haram have an exclusively Muslim following, the vast majority of Muslims would want to dissociate themselves from their activities. To insist that they are part of Islam is just as unreasonable as insisting that the IRA or the Ku Klux Klan (KKK) are part of Christianity, or that the Irgun, the Stern Gang and the Haganah are part of Judaism. All these groups certainly draw on their respective parent religions for membership, and all have agendas that are in some way associated with their religious identity. While Jewish Zionists may not necessarily practise Judaism as a religion, their cause is nonetheless associated with the religion's traditional teachings about a promised land that God purportedly gave to Abraham, and which was the Jewish homeland in biblical times.

If one looks at the Abrahamic religions as totalities, then of course all three faiths contain good and evil. In this section we agreed to focus on media portrayals, and the question we should be discussing is whether the media are more inclined to portray Muslims in a negative light, compared with Jews and Christians. The expressions 'Muslim terrorists', 'Islamic fundamentalists' and 'Islamic extremists' are frequently used in the media. One does not so frequently hear the terms 'terrorist' and 'extremist' used in conjunction with Judaism or Christianity. (The term 'fundamentalist', when applied to Christianity, carries a rather different meaning – that of a believer in biblical inerrancy, who does not necessarily support violence.)

I mentioned earlier the UK Press Complaints Commission's requirement that a person's religion should not be identified unless it is relevant to a story. Certainly in the case of the *Charlie Hebdo* killings, when the assassins left the newspaper's office shouting the Islamic acclamation 'Allahu Akbar!' ('God is great!'), it was relevant to identify them as Muslim. However, when *The Sun* published a front-page headline a few months earlier which read '"Muslim Convert" beheads woman', it was rightly criticised. How often do we read 'Church of England member guilty of murder' or 'Prominent Jew commits fraud', despite the fact that there are actually numerous incidents for which such headings could be appropriate? Understandably the Ku Klux Klan receives less news coverage in the media, but recent reports have highlighted its racist and violent nature, rather than its religious roots which are based on its distinctive understanding of the Bible.

How to persuade the media to give even-handed treatment to all three faiths is a difficult problem. In 2012 the Leveson Report on the British press accused the Press Complaints Commission of lack of independence and lack of disciplinary action against journalists and editors following upheld complaints. There is little evidence that the Independent Press Standards Organisation (IPSO), which replaced the PCC, is faring much better. No doubt politicians are wary of attempting to control the press, partly because few people would wish to see censorship, but perhaps more especially because political parties know only too well how the media can influence public opinion about them.

Dawoud   I am very much in agreement with George's view that we cannot hold the crimes of a relatively small number of people against entire faith communities, yet Dan is not wrong that there has been a terrifying explosion in the scale of violence perpetrated in the name of Islam in recent years. While the great majority of Muslims would not support the actions of terrorists, many feel that they are viewed with suspicion due to the relentless identification of Islam with terrorism in the media, and many may share the feelings of disempowerment and humiliation that have in part contributed to the current wave of radicalisation. As Dan also suggests, however, there are different viewpoints with regard to any act of terror. I have to emphasise that in no way would I ever condone any such groups or their actions, nor would the majority of Muslims, but sometimes we have to look at situations through the eyes of others, and through their own media which are as course as manipulative as our own (although not necessarily for the same commercial reasons) to understand what may drive them. Who is a terrorist? Who has the right to say who is a terrorist and who is not? Some might express the opinion that many parts of the Muslim world have been devastated over the last 25 years or so since Western powers started to tear down the puppet regimes that they had installed and used for decades to suppress their populations and facilitate the extraction of their natural resources. The invasion and war in Iraq are widely considered to have been illegal under international law and resulted in, at the lowest estimate, more than 100,000 violent civilian deaths. Here I think we have to look at the situation from the point of view of the 'general public', as Dan suggests, except that here the general public are not 'us' but the population of Iraq, and from the point of view of the innocent victims of the war, it is Bush and Blair who look very much like the terrorists. We refer to those who resisted the US-led invasion as 'insurgents', whereas if they were more 'like us' they might be considered to be 'resistance' or 'freedom fighters' striving for the liberation of their country from an invading foreign enemy. After the attacks on the World Trade Center in 2001, George Bush declared a 'crusade' against terror. This is a very loaded word for many Muslims and particularly the populations of the Middle East, to whom it sounded like the declaration of a holy war. If we are looking at the way conflicts are perceived, until the second half of the 20th century the mediaeval Crusades in Palestine and the Levant were portrayed in the West in literature and history books, in churches and schools, as the righteous actions of the civilised Christian world against the barbarous unbelievers, a perception that still permeates the subconscious of Western culture. To the populations of the region, however, they were and are understood as the aggressive actions of an invading foreign power.

We have to condemn any violent action, especially where it harms civilians and the innocent, but we should also be aware that our perception is not always the only valid one.

Dan   George and Dawoud seek to minimise the role of Islam in current outbursts of terrorist violence. George asks about the KKK: it must be remembered that they are a tiny fringe organisation, whereas Islamic jihadists represent a significant dimension within the Islamic world. Dawoud stresses that the majority of Muslims do not support the actions of terrorists. That may be so, but there is no doubt that the media are correct in identifying Muslims as responsible for crimes against humanity. Islamic jihadists themselves are adamant that their actions are driven by religious conviction. Although Dawoud is critical of such actions, he writes that 'we have to look at situations through the eyes of others'. He asks: 'Who has the right to say who is a terrorist and who is not?'

I could not disagree more. Western powers have been responsible for destabilising the Middle East region. Yet, this in no way exonerates jihadists for their terrorist campaign against the West. No doubt it was a mistake for President Bush to describe the war against terrorism as a crusade. It should be noted that he later apologised for this remark due to the negative connotations of the term. Britain itself announced publicly that it was abandoning use of the phrase 'War on Terror'.

Yet, whatever the policy is called, there is every reason for Western countries to seek to curtail terrorist activity. President Bush outlined a range of objectives in such a campaign:

- Defeat terrorists and demolish their organisations.

- Deny sponsorship, support and sanctuary to terrorists.

- Abolish terrorist sanctuaries and havens.

- Diminish the underlying conditions that terrorists seek to exploit.

- Partner with the international community to strengthen weak states and prevent the emergence of terrorism.

- Win the war of ideals. (Wikipedia 2016a)

Arguably these are justifiable aims given the danger that terrorism poses to peace and stability.

In this respect, the media has been right to draw attention to the dangers posed by Islamic terrorists throughout the world. Most recently, here in the United Kingdom, the BBC has revealed that at least 700 people from the UK have travelled to support or fight for jihadist organisations in Syria and Iraq. About half have since returned to Britain. Most of those who went to the conflict zone are thought to have joined the militant group that calls itself ISIS or IS. Such revelations are of critical importance in directing attention to deeply troubling problems within British society.

The media have also been instrumental in giving voice to such figures as Sarah Khan, the director of Inspire, who has encouraged young Muslim women not to travel to Syria. Her aim has been to mobilise women to challenge Islamic extremism. Her presence in the media has encouraged Muslim girls to resist extremist influences. The point is that the media play a critically important role in disseminating information about the dangers posed by terrorists, and provide a voice for those who seek to counter terrorist propaganda.

Dawoud is critical of the war against Iraq. He is right that the West has destabilised the region. But he is misguided in expressing empathy or sympathy for jihadists who use violence to gain their ends. Islamic terrorism currently poses the greatest threat to world stability and should be condemned. There is a holy war being fought against freedom and liberty – it is an Islamic crusade fuelled by hatred. Dawoud is wrong to suggest that there are other valid interpretations. There is only one correct perception of this evil – it is ours.

George   Dan seems to have reacted violently – metaphorically speaking, of course – to what Dawoud and I have said. However, it is not clear precisely what he is objecting to. So let me try to sum up the points on which we are agreed.

I think we might all agree that the Islamic religion is associated with terrorist organisations such as Al-Qaeda, Boko Haram and ISIS, and that they act for reasons connected to the Islamic faith. We might also agree, I think, that these terrorists have their reasons for acting as they do – they are not like vandals or street gangs, who commit acts of destruction and violence with no obvious motive. I think we agree too that we are in no way exonerating them in making this observation. None of us, I think, would wish to see the introduction of the kind of theocratic state for which ISIS aims, but even if this were a commendable aim, we could not condone the killing of innocent victims, the kidnappings that have occurred, or the destruction of ancient archaeological sites. All three of us are in accord that the majority of Muslims do not support the actions of ISIS. I am sure we are all agreed too that terrorism presents a serious danger, and that it must be combated, as Dan affirms. It seems, too, that all three of us would wish to be critical of the American and British invasion of Iraq, and recognise that such hostility was provocative, and contributed at least to some of the ensuing terrorism.

So where do we differ? I think a large measure of our disagreements lies in how we express our views on the so-called jihadists. Dan seems to insist that these terrorists are 'part of Islam', but I can only repeat my previous observation here that, whatever their relative sizes, they are no more 'part of Islam' than the Irgun, the Stern Gang and the Haganah are 'part of Judaism', or the IRA and the Ku Klux Klan are 'part of Christianity'. Religions are not like societies that issue membership cards, making it obvious who is in and who is out. Our respective religions as a whole contain such groups, but of course they do not necessarily reflect the teachings of their founder-leaders, or secure the assent of the majority of followers.

Unfortunately, in identifying these terrorist groups as 'Islamic extremists' or jihadists, the media readily convey the impression that Islam condones – even requires – such acts of violence. There is also an unevenness in the way terrorism is reported with respect to our three different faiths. As I pointed out, the media tend not to talk about Christian terrorism and, in the light of the traumatic history of the Jewish people, both the press and the public tend to be much more wary of appearing to be antisemitic (or, more precisely, anti-Jewish) than of expressing hostility to Islam.

When Iraq was invaded in 2003, the press did not call it a Christian invasion, although the invading countries – the US, UK, Australia and Poland – are all countries where the majority of the population are at least nominally Christian. Whether the invaders should have been called terrorists is debatable, of course. Dawoud said that Bush and Blair looked very *like* terrorists to the innocent war victims. The effects of their actions were certainly similar, but of course there are important differences between the actions of democratically elected governments and terrorist groups who lack any popular mandate. I raised the question earlier of whether a nation state might be described as 'terrorist', but to the victims the issue is an academic one.

Dawoud   I think George has summed up the discussion very effectively. To be clear, in case I have not emphasised this adequately so far, I do not excuse the barbaric actions of terrorists who commit atrocities against the innocent or who seek to impose a brutal totalitarian version of Islam that would be rejected by the majority of Muslims. Rightly, the media have highlighted the atrocities committed against vulnerable religious minorities including Christians and Yazidis under ISIS, but much less emphasis is placed on the fact that by far the greatest number of victims of the conflict are other Muslims, both Sunna and Shi'a, who do not conform to the fanatical ideals of ISIS. I have looked at some of the possible factors that historically may have been part of what has led us to this situation, including a sense of disempowerment and humiliation, but of course two wrongs never make a right.

There is in fact a '#notinmyname' movement which makes full use of social media to express the opposition of ordinary Muslims of all nationalities and ethnicities, men and women of all ages, to the actions and objectives of ISIS and other self-styled militant Islamic movements.

In online videos and other forums including Facebook and Twitter, they emphasise the fact that ISIS in no way represents them or the Islam that they know, which is a religion of peace and tolerance. Campaigns of this kind do not attract the same level of media attention as atrocities and acts of violence; we rarely find reports headed (for example) 'Muslim peace movement', yet the media are quick to use the terms, 'Islamic terrorism' or 'Muslim terrorists'. The prevalence of this point of view in the media promotes a distorted image of Islam and leads to a popular association of Muslims with terrorism, which in turn feeds into an Islamophobia which can make Muslims feel excluded and unfairly discriminated against. This is socially divisive and along with other xenophobic rhetoric and media manipulation, risks creating a segregated society where communities live in fear and suspicion of each other.

In the wake of the *Charlie Hebdo* killings in Paris in January 2015, the brother of the Muslim policeman Ahmed Merabet, who was murdered by the gunmen, spoke out saying:

> My brother was Muslim and he was killed by two terrorists, by two false Muslims. Islam is a religion of peace and love. As far as my brother's death is concerned it was a waste. He was very proud of the name Ahmed Merabet, proud to represent the police and of defending the values of the Republic – liberty, equality, fraternity.

He stressed that France, like the rest of Europe, faces a struggle against extremists, not against Muslims, saying:

> I address myself now to all the racists, Islamophobes and antisemites. One must not confuse extremists with Muslims. Mad people have neither colour or religion . . . I want to make another point: don't tar everybody with the same brush, don't burn mosques – or synagogues. You are attacking people. It will not bring back our loved ones and it will not bring peace to the families. (*The Observer*, 10 January 2015)

I would like to think the majority of Muslims and non-Muslims would agree.

CHAPTER 11

Free speech, blasphemy and religious hatred

We favour freedom of speech and expression, and react badly to suggestions that the press should be subject to greater state control. Yet it was the freedom of the press that gave rise to the Charlie Hebdo massacres. Does free speech have limits? Are blasphemy laws outmoded, and should we be prevented from inciting religious and racial hatred?

George   Dawoud's mention of *Charlie Hebdo* in the previous chapter serves as a good cue for our next topic, which is about blasphemy. There can be little doubt about the offensive nature of the cartoons that provoked the 2015 terrorist attack, although it should be noted that the *Charlie Hebdo* magazine does not exclusively target Muslims but publishes a range of satirical material. Of course, the editorial staff should have realised the risks they were running, particularly since they had been the target of a previous attack in 2011.

There can be little doubt that material that ridicules Muhammad or the Qur'an is deeply offensive to Muslims, even if the terrorists' reprisal was grossly disproportionate. The reaction to the attacks tended to polarise opinion, with many Muslims claiming that their religion had been blasphemed, while many others felt constrained to express solidarity with the journal, using the slogan 'Je suis Charlie', and championing freedom of speech and expression.

Herein lies the difficulty. Should freedom of expression include freedom to insult, to ridicule or to blaspheme, or should religious believers enjoy the right to follow their faith, free from harassment, ridicule and misrepresentation? Blasphemy is a religious offence, and does not of itself harm anyone apart from the blasphemer, so long as those who are likely to be offended do not have to read or view the offensive material.

In Britain, laws prohibiting blasphemy remained in force until very recently and, remarkably, there was a successful prosecution for this offence as late as 1976. In 2006 the British government attempted to steer a middle course by identifying incitement to religious hatred as the offence that ought to be outlawed by legislation. Religious hatred has consequences that go beyond its perpetrators, and differs from blasphemy, which may shock but not necessarily promote hatred.

When the the Racial and Religious Hatred Act 2006 was introduced, concerns were expressed that it might inhibit a number of acceptable practices relating to religion. The comedian Rowan Atkinson expressed concern that such an act might outlaw religious humour (BBC News Channel 2004). Few people would wish to see religion being taken so seriously as to disallow jokes or comic sketches. Equally, we would not wish to see an end to forceful debate between different religions, or criticism of beliefs and practices pertaining to faiths other than our own. Even expressing one's own faith can at times involve implicit criticism or contradiction of another: for example, Jews and Muslims, both of whom disallow the use of images, could be offended by the Christian use of statues or other art forms. Respect for other people's faith should not involve suppression of one's own.

Achieving this delicate balance between maintaining harmony between different faiths on the one hand, while allowing humour, criticism and debate on the other, is no easy task. Few people would want to see censorship, which would place both the media and religious organisations under state control. The 2006 act therefore strikes a balance between allowing freedom of expression, but requiring responsibility in the way one expresses one's views on religion. This is not to say that all is well with media portrayals of our faiths. On the contrary, as I have mentioned previously, the media – and particularly the tabloid press – have still a long way to go in ensuring responsible and accurate reporting of religious matters.

Dawoud The attack on the offices of *Charlie Hebdo* in January 2015 was an outrage carried out by terrorists with no justification, religious or otherwise; let me state that from the outset. While Muslims might feel offended by the nature of the cartoons, those who carried out this and other brutal attacks do far more damage to Islam than satirical words or images could ever do. I do not believe that freedom of speech should ever be curtailed because this would put us in the hands of the bullies. Muslims are quite happy to express their opinion that historically Jews and Christians falsified or at least altered their scriptures, yet they may react badly to any questioning of the text of the Qur'an or of the received history of early Islam. We cannot allow violence or the threat of violence to determine what we can and cannot say, and we have to believe that our own faiths are robust enough to withstand questioning and criticism. If we succumb to intimidation in this, then we make ourselves vulnerable to further threats as to what we can or cannot say or do.

I think we are entitled to discuss and to challenge other beliefs and doctrines honestly and openly, but at the same time most of us would be mortified if we felt that we had offended other people by our words and would do our best to avoid this.

There is, I believe, a sense that Muslims have no sense of humour, particularly when religion is involved, but this is really not the case. In July 2015 the first ever Muslim comedy festival 'Muslim Funny Fest' was held in New York with the aim of proving otherwise. Like most humour, however, the object of the humour of Muslim comedians is not so much the religion itself, but the human foibles of its adherents: weaknesses, pretensions and misunderstandings, intergenerational outwitting, and male–female dynamics – the themes are universal. It also explores the reactions and misunderstandings of others with whom Muslims interact and takes on issues of prejudice and preconception. Where many Muslims start to feel uncomfortable, offended, even enraged, however, is when satire appears to be more deliberately insulting and provocative. While satire can be an important tool in real and valid political and social commentary and criticism, it is difficult to know what purpose could be served by gross caricatures of the Prophet Muhammad such as the image of a stereotypical evil Arab with a bomb for a turban, other than establishing the right to offend. Such images are counter-productive in that they insult and alienate people rather than encourage them to examine real issues.

Dan   How can one balance the need to protect religious believers from discrimination and hatred while permitting legitimate criticism of religion? George is right to focus on the British government's legislation concerning this issue. The Equality Act was passed in 2006. This legislation makes it unlawful for someone to discriminate against another because of his or her religion or belief. This anti-discrimination requirement applies:

- in any aspect of employment

- when goods, facilities and services are being provided

- when education is being provided

- in using or disposing of premises

- when exercising public functions.

Under British anti-discrimination and human rights legislation, citizens are allowed to practise their religion or belief, to express their views, and to get on with their day-to day lives without experiencing threats or discrimination.

In the same year the British Parliament passed the Racial and Religious Hatred Act. This law forbids stirring up hatred against persons on racial or religious grounds. The Explanatory Notes to this law explain that:

> The new offences apply to the use of words or behaviour or display of written material, publishing or distributing written material, the public performance of a play, distributing, showing or playing a recording, broadcasting or including a programme in a programme service, and the possession of written materials or recordings with a view to display, publication, distribution or inclusion in a programme service. For each offence, the words, behaviour, written material, recordings or programmes must be threatening or intended to stir up religious hatred. Religious Hatred is defined as hatred against a group or person defined by reference to religious belief or lack of religious belief. (http://researchbriefings.parliament.uk/ResearchBriefing/Summary/SN03768)

Some time ago I was involved in a case that fell under this legislation. I acted as an expert witness for the Counter-Terror Division of the Crown

Prosecution Service. Two individuals were accused of disseminating antisemitic material on the internet. They did not seek to incite religious hatred against Jews; rather their attack was directed against Jews themselves. The question before the court was whether Jews constitute an ethnic group, and therefore whether these individuals could be prosecuted under this act for inciting racial hatred. (The definition of a racial group has been broadened in British law to include ethnic groups.) In the end, these individuals were found guilty and imprisoned.

I mention this case because it is directly relevant to the problem we are discussing. In Britain legitimate criticism of religious belief is permitted. Freedom of speech is paramount. But it is not unlimited. British law draws a line against the incitement of hatred against religion and members of ethnic groups. In the case of the Jewish community, if individuals deliberately seek to incite hatred of Judaism or Jews, they are subject to severe legal penalties. The same applies to other religious and ethnic communities. By contrast, the Nazis determinedly sought to encourage hatred of Jews and the Jewish faith. The Third Reich was a racial state, committed to eliminating undesirable elements from its midst. The Holocaust is a stark warning from history of the horror that human beings can unleash against those who adhere to religious convictions.

George   Near where I live, in the city of Lichfield, is a plaque commemorating the last person to be burnt at the stake for heresy – Edward Wightman, an Anabaptist clergyman who was executed in 1612 for denying the Trinity, among other key Christian doctrines. The intervening 400 years have seen tremendous liberalisation, and to impose legal sanctions for unpopular belief is now unthinkable in Western countries. But this liberalisation has also been coupled with a growing irreverence, and we live in a culture which has allowed Salman Rushdie's *The Satanic Verses*, the *Charlie Hebdo* magazine, *Jerry Springer: The Opera*, and Monty Python's *Life of Brian*.

Few people would like to see a 'nanny state' which decides on our behalf what we can read and what we can view. However, a number of European governments are of the opinion that there are limits. Some 14 European countries, including France and Germany, have introduced laws outlawing Holocaust denial, for example. This is a particularly difficult issue. On the one hand, a free society should be able to tolerate the expression of a variety of viewpoints on controversial issues, and particularly in our universities academic freedom is normally regarded as paramount. While academics welcome lively debate, we would not want courts of law to adjudicate on our ideas, or impose penalties on unpopular opinions. On the other hand, the vast majority of Jews find Holocaust denial to be deeply offensive, and the motives of many of the deniers are questionable, since their desire is often to stir up hatred rather than to engage in objective enquiry. Dan refers to the law's requirement that incitement to religious hatred must involve words or behaviour that are intended to foster hostility, but it is notoriously difficult to determine someone's intentions.

Holocaust deniers have sometimes been accused of having predetermined conclusions, but is not this equally true of those who affirm the Holocaust and do not wish to hear the deniers put their case? Deniers have been accused of using partial evidence rather than the whole story – for example claiming that there were not enough gas chambers to kill six million Jews. (This may or may not be true, but many victims died through other causes, such as starvation, dysentery and other forms of execution – which they tend not to mention.) However, many controversies feature incomplete evidence being given on both sides, and this justification for silencing the deniers would seem to preclude almost any debate on controversial subjects. Another justification for silencing the deniers lies in the way their opinions are expressed, for example when Ku Klux Klansmen appear in their hooded robes, making Nazi salutes, and bearing placards with slogans like 'Holocaust – gigantic Zionist hoax!', rational discussion can certainly be ruled out. However, the offence here surely lies in their provocative actions – which would be justifiably outlawed by recent British legislation – rather than in their opinions.

In suggesting that the right to freedom of speech might extend into discussion of the Holocaust, I am conscious of writing this with some trepidation. Of course the Jews were subjected to unprecedented suffering on a scale that is hard to imagine. While few of the victims are still alive, in many cases close friends and family remain, and their trauma can be exacerbated by those who deny it, trivialise it or ridicule it. How do we reconcile freedom of expression with the need for respect and sensitivity?

Dawoud   When I was growing up in Egypt, it was a popular belief expressed without reservation or embarrassment that the Holocaust was a story exaggerated by the West as propaganda to create sympathy for Jews and to justify the occupation of Palestine and the displacement of hundreds of thousands of Palestinians from their villages and towns. It is as if by denying the death and suffering of millions of Jews, the suffering of the Palestinians would seem somehow more atrocious, or as if the horrors of the Holocaust were somehow cancelled out by what was subsequently done to the Palestinians, and the Jews of Europe were thereby not deserving of sympathy. While the expression of such ideas is deeply offensive, it is difficult to define why, exactly, one such discrete notion should be singled out for specific legislation. I think the answer to this, as George has touched upon, is that Holocaust denial does not appear to be straightforward, unbiased, academic debate amongst historians but emerges out of hatred. It is a form of antisemitism and a deliberate slander against the Jewish people, aimed at inciting racial and religious hatred. Such calumnies repeated often enough can develop a life of their own.

The same kind of propaganda appears in the variously attributed expression 'a land without people for a people without land', which became popular amongst both Zionists and Christian Restorationists of the 19th and early 20th centuries. As Golda Meir told *The Sunday Times* in 1969, 'There is no such thing as a Palestinian people . . . It is not as if we came and threw them out and took their country. They didn't exist'. It has been part of the State of Israel's propaganda to deny the national existence of the Palestinians. This is the same kind of wilful misinformation designed to diminish the humanity of 'the other', for while Palestine might not have been a nation state with a fully formed identity, this does not mean that the people and communities of Palestine did not exist. Their national identity, like that of many other peoples including the Israelis, has been forged in adversity.

Like George, I am wary of any form of censorship or restriction on what we may or may not say because restriction of freedom of speech is the first step on the road to the closing down of other freedoms. To be able to challenge everything with our words and to be challenged is a fundamental part of our democracy, and the countries which are the most restrictive of freedom of expression, religious or secular, are those where most of us would least like to live. Words are powerful. Words can be weapons and they can be used for good or ill. People of religion may feel wounded by malicious, or even just careless words, but the answer cannot be to counter these with violence. They should be countered with better words. Words have the power to incite hatred and violence, but they also have the power to inspire and to liberate.

Dan   There is no doubt that, as Dawoud pointed out, Holocaust denial is motivated by hatred of Jews. As you know, in some countries it is forbidden by law. Personally, I think this is an overreaction. It is far better, I believe, to counter Holocaust denial through evidence and argument. But I want to address the issue that Dawoud refers to concerning the existence of the Palestinian people. It is true that some early Zionists claimed that Palestine in the 19th century was a land without people. This false assertion was made – not because of hatred of the indigenous Arab population – but to support the Zionism cause.

It was of course untrue, and there were leading Zionist figures who were anxious to refute it. The great Russian essayist, Ahad Ha-Am, for example, recognised at the end of the 19th century that the Arab Palestinians might press for the creation of a national movement. It is a mistake, he argued, to believe that Palestine is devoid of a native population. He wrote:

> We tend to believe abroad that Palestine is nowadays almost completely deserted, a non-cultivated wilderness, and anyone can come there and buy as much land as his heart desires. But in reality this is not the case. It is difficult to find anywhere in the country Arab land which lies fallow. (Avineri 1981/1984:122)

According to Ahad Ha-Am, what is required is a sense of realism. Jews should not regard themselves as superior to their Arab neighbours. Instead they should perceive that the Arabs are fiercely proud and determined:

> We tend to believe abroad that all Arabs are desert barbarians, an asinine people who do not see or understand what is going on around them. This is a cardinal mistake ... The Arabs, and especially the city dwellers, understand very well what we want and what we do in the country; but they behave as if they do not notice it because at present they do not see any danger for themselves or their future

in what we are doing and are therefore trying to turn to their benefit these new guests . . . But when the day will come in which the life of our people in the land of Israel will develop to such a degree that they will push aside the local population by little or much, then it will not easily give up its place. (Avineri 1981/1984:123)

In order to flourish in the land of their ancestors, Ahad Ha-Am insisted that the Jewish people act with love and respect towards those Arabs in their midst.

Other early Zionists were similarly aware of the necessity of recognising the needs and rights of their Arab neighbours. The organisation Brit Shalom was founded in the 1930s by a group of universalist Jewish intellectuals including Martin Buber, Albert Einstein and Gershom Scholem who sought a peaceful co-existence with the Arab population. This was to be achieved by renouncing the Zionist aim of creating a Jewish state. Following the vision of Ahad Ha-Am, it advanced an alternative Zionist concept of creating a centre for Jewish cultural life in Palestine. In their view, what was required was a bi-national state in which Jews and Arabs would live in peace and harmony with one another. The tragedy is that the history of Israel followed another course, and that in the process there has been an ongoing bloody struggle between two peoples.

CHAPTER 12

Religious humour

Most of us enjoy a good joke. But when does a joke go too far? Many religious believers take the view that their faith is a serious matter, and should certainly not be mocked – an opinion shared by the Charlie Hebdo *assassins. In what circumstances is it acceptable to laugh at someone's faith, and does it make a difference whether it is our own faith or someone else's?*

Dawoud   As early as the 9th century CE we find examples of Muslim writers producing works of humour and satire. Al-Jahiz, for example, produced works of literature, theology and politics, but amongst his best known writings is his Kitab al-Bukhala or Book of Misers. This pokes fun at the greed and miserliness of all kinds of people, including schoolmasters, singers and scribes. The humour is gentle and humane and presents the misers as foolish rather than wicked. The stories are amusing because we recognise some of the traits of the characters, and they are mildly didactic. Al-Jahiz lived during the period of the Abbasids at a time of dynamic cultural exchange and development and his stories are well known and still widely reproduced today.

Throughout the Middle East stories have been told for centuries of a folk character called Joha in Arab countries or Goha in Egypt, and Mullah Nasruddin or Nasruddin Khoja in Persia and Turkey. He is also known by other names further afield. Many of the stories are old and well known, but sometimes they are reworked in different environments and contexts and new ones appear. Joha is part fool, part sage and the humorous short tales told about him are sometimes absurd, sometimes ironic, and sometimes offer comment on manners, society and politics in ways that would not be possible in any other form.

Personally I think religious humour can be extremely funny, but as I have already mentioned, I think this is because the best of it is generally about people and not about religion itself. The finest humour looks at the human fallibilities which all of us share irrespective of faith. It holds a mirror to society and enables us all to recognise our own weaknesses and failings, selfishness, hypocrisy, self-righteousness, pretension and pomposity, and it can challenge stereotyping and discrimination.

At the same time, however, jokes can be malicious and deliberately hurtful. A brief search of the internet will throw up many offensive jokes which are not funny but simply gratuitous jibes at an entire community. They seem to fall into several general categories: a great number are centred on a basic premise that associates Muslims with bombs and beheadings or infers an entire faith is composed of violent psychopaths, some attack Muslim belief and practice (or some distorted view of these), some mock the dress or names of Muslims, some accuse them of being lechers and paedophiles, and some simply accuse Muslims of poor personal hygiene. There is really nothing funny in any of this, and it is hard to imagine that it would be in any way acceptable to make similar jokes about any other religious or racial group.

It is conventionally held that the best Jewish jokes are told by Jews, and I think the same is generally true for Muslims, and probably all other faith groups. When communities make jokes about themselves, it is done with affection and self-awareness, and when it is shared with others it may give an insight into their common humanity.

Dan   A Jewish joke:

> After a long illness, Harold Goldberg died aged 92. His wife phoned the local Jewish newspaper, and asked if she could put in an announcement about her husband's death. 'There is a charge for this', the editor said. 'How much?', Mrs Goldberg asked. 'Well, the cheapest is £100 for five words.' There was a pause. Eventually Mrs. Goldberg said: 'What about "Goldberg dead". Is there a discount?' 'Sorry', said the editor, 'the price is the same whether it's two or five words'. Mrs. Goldberg went silent. 'OK', she finally said, 'what about: "Goldberg dead. Volvo for sale"?'.

Jews are used to making jokes about themselves. There is a long tradition of humour in Judaism, dating back to the Torah and the Midrash. The Bible itself recounts how Sarah laughed when told she would have a child, and Isaac is named for that laughter. The Talmud, particularly in aggadic passages, is replete with witty asides and repartees. During the medieval period, humour was institutionalised in various customs, perhaps most famously in Purim *shpiels*, comic plays based on the book of Esther.

In the 19th century, the Jewish joke developed into its own recognisable species. The shtetl (Jewish village) became home for the Jewish humour folk tradition – stories of fools inhabiting the town of Chelm are an example. Jewish writers including Mendele Mokher Seforim and Sholem Aleichem produced lasting classics of Jewish humour. In modern times, humour has played a central role in Jewish life. Beginning with vaudeville and continuing through stand-up comedy, film and television, Jews have been known for their ability to make audiences laugh. In many cases the primary aim has been to mock Jewish stereotypes.

Paradoxically, humour has enabled Jews to endure the most horrific circumstances throughout their long history. As the novelist Saul Bellow pointed out, oppressed people tend to be witty – through the centuries Jews developed humour as a way of living with their hardships. Yet there is more to humour than dealing with persecution and suffering. Jews value learning, and the tradition of questioning and challenging religious authorities extends into humour as a means of puncturing pomposity.

In general Jewish humour is all about coping. Sigmund Freud wrote that he did not know whether there were other instances of a people making fun of its own character. Other commentators suggested the Jewish jest is a survival tactic: by altering one's perspective, the Jew can accept the unsympathetic world for what it is. Given the centrality of humour in the Jewish community, it is difficult to understand why members of other faiths (particularly Muslims) are offended by jokes about their tradition. No Jew would be offended by jokes about Abraham or Moses or the rabbis. Such as:

> A rabbi dies and is waiting in line to enter heaven. In front of him is a man dressed in a loud shirt, leather jacket, jeans and sunglasses.

Gabriel says to the man, 'I need to know who you are so that I can determine whether or not to admit you to the kingdom of heaven'. The man replies, 'I'm Moishe Levy, taxi driver'. Gabriel consults his list, smiles and says to the taxi driver, 'OK. Take this silken robe and golden staff and enter the kingdom of heaven'. Now it's the rabbi's turn. He stands upright and says, 'I am Benjamin Himmelfarb and I have been a rabbi for 40 years'. Gabriel looks at his list and says to the rabbi, 'OK. Take this cotton robe and wooden staff and enter the kingdom of heaven'. 'Hold on a minute', says Rabbi Himmelfarb, 'that man before me was a taxi driver. Why did he get a silken robe and golden staff?' 'Up here, we only work by results', says Gabriel, 'while you preached, people slept – but while he drove, people prayed'.

George Dan is right – there is quite a lot of laughter in the Bible, including 'laughter in heaven' (Psalm 2:4), although perhaps the divine laughter is derisory rather than witty here! Certainly Jesus made the occasional joke. For example, talking about the camel going through the eye of a needle and the man with the plank in his eye criticising the person with a speck in his would no doubt get a laugh from his hearers (Mark 10:25; Luke 6:41–42). Gross exaggerations are characteristic of Mediterranean humour, and if we don't roll around laughing at them in the West today, this merely shows that senses of humour are culturally determined.

Humour can be a good way of making a point, teaching a topic or diffusing an embarrassing situation. To say 'I haven't even started drinking yet!' after tripping on a step might help to save my embarrassment, although maybe I should think twice before making such a comment in front of teetotallers, or even Muslims. However, if I were to make a comment suggesting that Muhammad had been drinking, this would be unspeakable – one of the reasons why Muslims found Salman Rushdie's *The Satanic Verses* thoroughly offensive.

Must religion be so serious that people of faith can't take a joke at their own expense? As Dawoud suggests, much depends on where the humour is coming from, what its motives are, and what effect it is likely to have. I like Dan's joke – although perhaps I would have hesitated to make it myself, in case it reinforced a stereotype. Dawoud's earlier reference in Chapter 11 to the New York 'Muslim Funny Fest' ably demonstrates that Muslims can laugh at themselves too, and as for Muslim humour I would also recommend *The Little Mosque on the Prairie* to readers who have not yet discovered it (accessible online at https://www.youtube.com/watch?v=_I4YrgGHCXE). The ability to laugh at oneself can be healthy and cause followers of the religion not to take themselves or their religious obligations over-seriously.

Dawoud rightly draws attention to inappropriate humour, which can fuel hatred and bigotry. In his book *The Nature of Prejudice* (1954), sociologist Gordon Allport identified five stages of hostility towards vulnerable communities: antilocution, avoidance, discrimination, physical attack and extermination. By 'antilocution' Allport means that opposition tends first to be expressed in verbal abuse, insults and hostile jokes. This may be followed by the oppressed group being avoided or marginalised, which may in turn lead to discrimination, especially in employment and education, and subsequently to more violent forms of opposition – in the case of Nazi Germany the aim of total extermination of Jews. Inappropriately directed, hostile humour can be the vehicle for initiating and unleashing prejudice and even violence.

This is not to imply that we should not make jokes about religion or about faith groups. This would be as much of an over-reaction as to suggest that we should not drive a car because cars can kill people. What it does indicate is that, as with driving one's car, we need to exercise due caution. The *Charlie Hebdo* staff were clearly aware of the gross inflammatory nature of their material, and the consequences – although unjustifiable – were not unexpected. I don't think it is a sufficient justification to say that such material is in the 'French satirical tradition' as some *Charlie Hebdo* supporters argued. Good satire has always served a definite purpose, and if humour can only be enjoyed by the dominant culture there ought to be cause for concern.

Dawoud   Laughter is universal and Muslims are essentially no different to anyone else when it comes to sense of humour, although the kind of humour that any society enjoys is of course tuned by culture and the nature of comedy will vary from one Muslim country to another.

It would, however, be unrealistic to deny that there is a strand of Islam that frowns upon excessive or improper laughter whatever the subject matter. Salafi and Wahhabi Islam and some communities influenced by them have a somewhat puritanical stance on humour, advocating the importance of taking life seriously and pointing to selected *hadith* that suggest that the Prophet disapproved of excessive jesting and laughter. From the *hadith* they extract a number of guidelines for humour and limits that should not be transgressed. According to these, jokes should not insult anyone, tricks and practical jokes should not frighten anyone, jokes should not be based on lies or untruth, joking should not be excessive for fear that it may cause people to lose the respect of others, and because people may lose focus on the fact that this life is temporary and true joy is to come in the next. Most of all, many Muslims including those who otherwise have a sense of humour will be deeply offended by jokes or cartoons that appear to mock or attack their faith or that they consider insulting to the Prophet due to the great love and esteem in which he is held.

This does not mean that Muslims cannot laugh at themselves. George refers to the Canadian sitcom *The Little Mosque on the Prairie* which portrays the life of a small Muslim community in a small town in Saskatchewan. The characters are mostly a mixture of generic ethnically middle-eastern Muslims, some immigrant and some Canadian born, religious and secular plus the occasional convert, an assortment of bigots and the misinformed and a friendly minister who is supportive of the Muslim community. Like a lot of contemporary Muslim humour, the show pokes fun at stereotypes, bigotry and ignorance, amongst the Muslim characters as well as the non-Muslims. It does not ridicule religion, but it laughs, rather gently, at the everyday foibles of the characters and the misunderstandings that they fall into. In common with the material of many Muslim stand-up comedians, it deals particularly with the everyday discrimination and profiling that Muslims experience, the way that people look at them with suspicion and fear on public transport or simply expect them to be different or alien to themselves.

Ten years or so ago whilst leading a field trip to Egypt, I overheard one of the mature students say to the student seated next to him on the bus that took us around Cairo: 'They look quite happy really, don't they?' It was a priceless moment that made the few of us who heard it look at each other and have to suppress our laughter but at the same time it filled me with a kind of despair at the thought that people might imagine that another community might be completely unlike them and that they were surprised that people were not innately miserable but going about their daily business just as they would anywhere else.

Dan   George is right: if he – as a non-Jew – were to tell the joke I told in the last exchange, this would be viewed as downright offensive. It is perfectly acceptable for Jews to tell jokes about themselves. Many are really awful, illustrating our foibles, prejudices and weaknesses. The worse they are, the funnier. Rabbis in particularly are much ridiculed. Biblical characters like Moses are also targets of fun. We Jews curl up with amusement. No one is outraged. No one is upset. We laugh, and laugh and laugh. But . . . if a non-Jew dares tell the same jokes, we are deeply insulted. The goyim (non-Jews) are not allowed to mock us. Instead we are quick to call in the Anti-Defamation League. We phone our lawyers. We consult community leaders. We summon the police. We cry 'hate crime'! We are UPSET!

It is a strange paradox. From within the community everything is a target for amusement. We absolutely adore ridiculing Jewish princesses, awful mothers-in-law, greedy businessmen, pompous rabbis, horrible children. The worse the jokes, the better. On the internet there are literally thousands of Jewish jokes about all aspects of Jewish life. We don't seem to care what we say. But this is a privilege reserved for Jews alone. If a non-Jew dares to cross the line and enter into the fun, he is branded an antisemite. A Jew-hater. An enemy of the Jewish people.

So George, and Dawoud, you are not permitted to join in the fun. I suppose it is OK if you laugh at Jewish jokes. But not too much. Just a bit. Just so we see that you are good fellows and can go along with our mockery and satire. But don't think you will ever be permitted to be comedians at our expense. We will pursue you through the courts, and aim to get you locked up for breaking the Racial and Religious Hatred Act 2006.

This is a puzzle I can't really explain. For thousands of years we Jews have been spat at and hated. This was particularly so in Christian countries. Viewed as Christ-killers, we suffered contempt, persecution and murder. In Muslim lands we were viewed as second-class citizens. Today we live in the shadow of the Holocaust. We have created a Jewish state in Palestine to protect ourselves from future aggression. No matter how secure we feel in the diaspora, we are conscious that our situation is unstable. As I noted in my last exchange, Jewish humour has enabled us to survive this precarious position. It is a strange antidote to hatred. We mirror Jewish stereotypes in the jokes we tell about each other.

But when others do this, the clouds darken. We feel surrounded by our enemies. Memories of distant centuries when our ancestors were threatened and killed come to haunt us. Non-Jewish laughter at our expense recalls the horrors of our past. It is somehow cathartic when we laugh at ourselves. But when others laugh at us, ridicule us and stereotype us, we are in fear of our lives. Images of the Holocaust close in on us, and we are filled with terror.

George   Since we seem to be telling jokes in this section, let me try a Christian one – or maybe it's very un-Christian!

> A man has a withered hand. 'You should go to Lourdes', a friend advises. 'People receive miraculous cures there.' The man goes to Lourdes, but comes back with two withered hands. 'What happened?' his friend asks. 'Well, I made a little mistake when saying my prayer. I said "Please God, make this hand like the other one!" But I held up the wrong hand!'

I have learnt to exercise care if I'm tempted to tell this joke. I once told it to a Protestant fundamentalist, only to be met with a stony silence.

I must confess that the idea of a God who works healing miracles but nonetheless takes prayer requests so literally as to disadvantage a devotee so seriously, strikes me as very funny indeed. However, my fundamentalist acquaintance no doubt felt it was subjecting one of Jesus' healing miracles to ridicule (Mark 3:1–5). Equally, Roman Catholics might take exception to the reference to Lourdes, and I guess some people might find the reference to disability offensive. So apologies to readers who are not amused!

I learned quite a few jokes like this as a church student, many years ago, and the fact that they therefore have Christian origins makes me more favourably disposed towards them. Like Dan, I am not sure how I would feel if a follower of some other faith told them. I would certainly not tell them if I thought my personal safety was at risk, but it is unlikely that even the members of Westboro Baptist Church would break into my house armed with semi-automatic rifles in retaliation.

When I served on the United Reformed Church's Other Faiths' Committee, the subject of religious humour once came up, and one member suggested writing some guidelines on the topic. I don't know if he ever did, but – for what they are worth – let me add one or two more to Dawoud's:

- Who 'owns' the humour? As Dan remarks, jokes told about one's own community are less likely to be taken amiss than those about others.

- Err on the side of caution. If it is likely that one's humour will be taken amiss, hold back!

- Is the joke's author laughing *at* or laughing *with* the faith community?

- Is the religious community a vulnerable group, and is there a likelihood that jokes at their expense might encourage prejudice, reinforce stereotypes or even provoke violence?

- How funny is the joke really? Obviously there are no agreed standards of hilarity, but if the humour falls short of strict standards of political correctness, the joke needs to be justified in terms of its funniness.

- To what extent does the humour make a point? Might a serious purpose underlie it, or is it simply gratuitously offensive? (Perhaps my Lourdes joke invites us to consider whether healing miracles really happen, or how God answers prayers. I don't know.) If humour is genuine satire rather than gratuitously offensive ridicule, then there may be more justification for putting it into the public domain.

I don't think the *Charlie Hebdo* staff met these criteria in their anti-Muslim humour, since much of it appears to have been gratuitously offensive. Where legal boundaries should be drawn is a difficult question, of course. We should not allow the terrorists to dictate what we laugh at, but on the other hand one should not cause such offence to the extent that it invites terrorism.

CHAPTER 13

Apocalyptic expectations

Some religious believers expect an imminent end to human affairs in a cosmic battle such as Armageddon. Armed conflict has typically been regarded as one of the signs of the end, so perhaps we are giving God a helping hand by provoking violence. Perhaps humankind's only hope is supernatural intervention?

Dan In 70 CE the Romans crushed the Jewish rebellion in Judaea, destroyed the Temple and drove the Jews out of Jerusalem. For the next two millennia Jews were without a homeland, compelled to live as aliens in foreign lands. Deprived of our ancient home, we prayed to God for deliverance. According to rabbinic Judaism, a human Messiah will eventually come to bring about the return of Jewish exiles back to Zion. Miraculously, the dead will be resurrected and transported to the Holy Land. During the Days of the Messiah (*Yamot Ha-Mashiah*), the Temple will be restored and there will be peace on earth. Eventually there will be a final judgement, and all human beings will either be rewarded or condemned everlastingly. The righteous will enter heaven (*Gan Eden*) and the wicked will be cast into hell (*Gehinnom*). This apocalyptic vision sustained the Jewish people through trials and tribulations for centuries.

Today most Jews have abandoned this eschatological scheme. Secular Jews in the diaspora and Israel do not anticipate messianic deliverance. At the end of the 19th century Zionists like Theodor Herzl were adamant: in their view the Jewish people must return to their ancestral home *en masse*. Only in this way will they be able to escape from the perils of antisemitism. They must constitute the majority in Israel if they are to free themselves from discrimination, persecution and murder. Reform

Jews similarly rejected the belief in messianic deliverance. In their view longing for supernatural intervention has been a misguided delusion.

There has thus been a major reversal in Jewish life and thought. Strictly Orthodox Jews continue to pray daily for the Messiah. But the vast majority of Jews have distanced themselves from this apocalyptic hope. Both secular and Progressive Jews are united in their conviction that peace, justice and harmony can only come about through human effort. This shift away from traditional Jewish belief constitutes a major revolution. The belief in messianic deliverance has been jettisoned in favour of humanistic values.

Such a reversal has widespread implications as far as the State of Israel is concerned. In the past Jews turned to God in times of despair. The belief in divine intervention sustained them in the face of suffering. Assured of divine deliverance and reward in the hereafter, they faced death with faith and hope. Today, however, such optimism has faded. Instead of relying on divine protection, Jews believe that the creation of a nation state in the Holy Land offers security and will ensure the survival of the Jewish nation and the Jewish faith.

This is nothing less than a modern form of paganism. It is not God who will save us from our enemies but the land of Israel. The nation state that we have created has become the ultimate insurance policy. It is sacred soil. Paradoxically, we Jews have invested a political entity with the attributes we previously ascribed to God. In this respect we have become worshippers of land which we have safeguarded with soldiers and tanks and nuclear warheads. In the shadow of the Holocaust, we have created a protective shield in the belief that it can ensure our survival. It is not God who will ultimately save his chosen people. Instead we ourselves can accomplish this with our own might and power. In this way we are responding to the Nazi nightmare of annihilation and extinction.

George   I clearly recall being in church on the Sunday after the Six Day War ended in 1967. I was quite young at the time, and felt enormously relieved that a third world war had been avoided. In his sermon the preacher declared how overjoyed he was to see the Jews enter Jerusalem and gain control of the holy city once again. Despite my youth, I was shocked. How could anyone – least of all a Christian minister – condone such an invasion?

Christian Zionism has been in existence for significantly longer than its Jewish counterpart, stemming from the migration of some of the Puritans from England to the United States, and gaining momentum through America's political interests in the Middle East. The Christian fundamentalists of the late 19th century believed that the Jews would return to their homeland as a fulfilment of biblical prophecy: God had promised Abraham that all the families of the earth would be blessed by his descendants (Genesis 12:7), and that King David's kingdom would be an everlasting kingdom (Psalm 145:13). The Balfour Declaration of 1917, which promised a homeland for the Jews, and the establishment of the State of Israel in 1948, gave further impetus to the movement.

Some Christian Zionists held that the return of the Jews would herald their acceptance of Jesus Christ as the Messiah, and would be a prelude to Christ's second coming, which would be followed by the Battle of Armageddon. Some expected that the Jerusalem Temple would be rebuilt, necessitating the demolition of the Dome of the Rock, much cherished by Muslims. The bestselling series of apocalyptic novels by the American fundamentalist authors Tim LaHaye and Jerry B. Jenkins, the first of which was published in 1995, and whose sales have exceeded 65 million copies, is an imaginative recounting of events following the Rapture, in which Jesus Christ takes his followers up to heaven, enabling them to avoid the ensuing tribulations on earth. The Jews are portrayed as having a key role in these end-time events, which include the Temple's restoration. It has been estimated that 63% of white evangelical Christians espouse some form of Zionism.

I believe these ideas are extremely dangerous. They have encouraged American pro-Israeli policies, which have included the appropriation of territory belonging to Palestinians, driving many from their homes. The belief that the Battle of Armageddon is inevitable militates against peace making: why make peace if large-scale war is necessary to accomplish God's purposes? By using God's name to advance their favoured material purposes, Christian Zionists violate the third commandment, 'You shall not misuse the name of the Lord your God' (Exodus 20:7).

Fortunately, Christian Zionism has many opponents. In 2006 the Jerusalem Declaration on Christian Zionism was signed jointly by the

Latin Patriarch of Jerusalem, the Syrian Orthodox Patriarch of Jerusalem, the Bishop of the Episcopal Church of Jerusalem and the Middle East, and the Bishop of the Evangelical Lutheran Church in Jordan and the Holy Land. They affirmed:

> We reject the teachings of Christian Zionism that facilitate and support these policies as they advance racial exclusivity and perpetual war rather than the gospel of universal love, redemption and reconciliation taught by Jesus Christ. Rather than condemn the world to the doom of Armageddon we call upon everyone to liberate themselves from ideologies of militarism and occupation. Instead, let them pursue the healing of the nations! (Sizer, 2013)

Dawoud   There is a vision of the Apocalypse in Islamic theology, although it is made very clear in the Qur'an that the time of its advent is known only to God. No human being, not even the Prophet Muhammad, can advance or delay it. The signs of the end time are various and include war and disaster, decadence and dishonesty, the abandoning of prayer, the spread of usury and fornication, and other immoral acts. A character known as Al-Massih Ad-Dajjal, the false Messiah, will appear spreading corruption and enticing people away from faith, and Jesus and the Mahdi will return to fight and conquer him before the final hour. After the tribulations, on the Day of Judgement, the dead will be resurrected and judged and only the true believers will go to heaven while the wicked will be burnt in hell. The Qur'an speaks frequently of the Day of Judgement and of reward and punishment in the hereafter, but the eschatology is found in more detail in the Hadith, and there are variations between the Sunna and the Shi'a.

Since the 1980s there has been a huge explosion in popular 'end time' literature of a kind comparable in its popularity and influence to the Christian Evangelical works of Hal Lindsey. David Cook, the foremost authority on contemporary Islamic apocalyptic writing, suggests that this entire genre was effectively created by the Egyptian journalist, Said Ayyub, who wrote a book in 1987 called *Al-Masih Al-Dajjal* (translated as *The Antichrist*) which interpreted current world events in the light of Islamic eschatology, describing the United States as the Great Satan (Cook, 2008). Ayyub based his work on material from the Islamic primary sources, along with the spurious Protocols of the Elders of Zion (refuted as a malicious antisemitic fabrication as early as 1920 in Europe but still widely circulated and believed in the Middle East), along with Christian millenarian and Christian Zionist material. Throughout this genre, the conspiracy theory focuses on Israel and world Jewry's aim of world domination, and the foreign policy of the United States.

In the same way that Hal Lindsey's writings and other evangelical material has permeated communities and popular culture, so has the notion of the Apocalypse fed into popular Muslim thought. There is little doubt that it has played a significant role in the rise of movements such as ISIS. In the light of identified signs of the end of the world, it is important to be on the side of the righteous fighting against the infidel. As they see things, since the decline of the Ottoman Empire leading to the fall of the Caliphate in 1924, Islam has been humiliated and oppressed and it is the duty of Muslims to restore Islam's power and prestige.

Cook suggests that this is related to the early history of Islam and its expansion under the Islamic conquests of the 7th and 8th centuries. Historians may argue that the expansion was based primarily on economic driving factors, but according to received history the motivation was essentially absolute faith and the desire to bring the world under Islam. What is important is that most Muslims today believe that faith was the key motivation. Cook argues that even this is not enough to explain the astonishing progress of the early conquests which were driven by the belief in the imminent Apocalypse and the need to conquer the world for Islam before the Day of Judgement. He suggests that the same beliefs are a key element motivating military jihad in the present.

Dan Dawoud has given a fascinating account of the apocalyptic vision of contemporary Islam. Similarly, George has provided an arresting insight into the mindset of Christian Zionists. It is clear that many Christians and Muslims are deeply influenced by such theories concerning the end time. Here theology and political action are intertwined. Within the Jewish community, however, it is only the strictly Orthodox (along with some believers in other branches of Judaism) who subscribe to similar messianic beliefs. As I mentioned previously, Reform Judaism, for example, has eliminated references to a personal Messiah from the liturgy. This is official policy and has been so for over a century.

What this means in effect is that contemporary Judaism has increasingly become a this-worldly faith which focuses on the importance of living a religious life in the here and now. In the past the belief in heavenly reward and eternal punishment was a cardinal feature of the tradition. In the Middle Ages the philosopher Moses Maimonides listed it as one of the thirteen cardinal principles of Judaism. Through the centuries this belief animated Jewish life and thought. Jews prayed daily for the coming of the Messiah and the beginning of the Messianic Age. But in the modern world this apocalyptic hope has largely faded from Jewish life.

This is nothing less than a revolution. In the past Jewish believers were persuaded that God would eventually redeem his people and restore them to the Holy Land. For nearly two thousand years our ancestors were consoled by the conviction that the Messiah will eventually triumph and Israel's enemies will be vanquished. Belief in bodily resurrection and eternal reward provided a source of consolation for those who suffered discrimination, persecution and murder. The innocent went to their deaths believing in ultimate redemption.

For the vast majority of Jews this is no longer the case. Instead we believe that, although God is present in our lives, he will not miraculously intervene in human history. There will be no Messiah. Nor will we be redeemed *en masse* and miraculously transported to Zion. The Temple will not be restored. Nor will we live through a period of messianic redemption in which peace and harmony will be established.

Instead, it is our religious responsibility to live Jewish lives in the here and now. Across the Jewish religious spectrum, this is understood in different ways. For the Orthodox a Jewish life consists in observing the *mitzvot* (divine commandments). In progressive branches of Judaism (Conservative, Reform, Liberal, Reconstructionist and Humanistic), a Jewish life is understood in other ways. In addition, dedication to the State of Israel is paramount. For the majority of Jews – religious and secular – a Jewish state is viewed as vital to Jewish existence. Without modern Israel, both Jews and Judaism are endangered.

Here then is a fundamental shift away from traditional apocalyptic thought. For Jews in Israel and the diaspora the apocalyptic aspirations of past ages have been superseded by the determination to ensure the survival of the Jewish state in our ancient homeland. Yet paradoxically we are surrounded by enemies whose belief in the end time envisages the destruction and elimination of a Jewish presence in the Holy Land.

George   Dawoud mentions apocalyptic visions, and I agree that these need to be treated with caution and responsibility. The Bible mentions an array of phenomena – some of which are violent – which are associated with the end times: wars, broken human relationships, signs in the heavens, the rapture of the faithful, a great tribulation, Christ's coming in the clouds, the last judgement, the Antichrist, the mark of the beast, Armageddon, a general resurrection, the millennium, the binding and release of Satan, and the New Jerusalem, among others.

These are not mentioned in one single passage, and are not placed chronologically. This has caused authors like LaHaye and Jenkins to beachcomb the Bible for clues about the last days, and to write novels that run counter to the vast majority of self-respecting scholars' biblical interpretation. Unfortunately, professional scholarly interpretation tends not to percolate down to the average believer. I can't set the record straight in one short section, but I can try to drop a hint or two about how biblical apocalyptic literature might be properly understood.

Despite LaHaye and Jenkins' biblical fundamentalism, they surreptitiously introduce non-biblical material into their novels. For example, the Bible never identifies the Antichrist – who, contrary to popular understanding, is never mentioned in the Book of Revelation – as a person. The restored Jerusalem Temple, which suddenly appears in the series without explanation, reflects a non-biblical expectation that the personified Antichrist would become an object of devotion there. The authors also imply that the Book of Revelation is a cryptic foretelling of world events from the time of Jesus into the present day and beyond, and that they are performing the service of unravelling its enigmas.

We need to question all of these assumptions. The belief that John the Revelator was predicting world events can be traced back at least as far as Joachim of Fiore (c.1132–1202) and this interpretation gained popularity under Protestant Reformers such as Wycliffe, Luther and Isaac Newton. However, it is unlikely that such long-term predictions would have helped the persecuted churches of the 1st century whom he was addressing. It is much more likely that the book's symbolism depicts these early Christians under Roman persecution, offering them encouragement to persevere, with the prospect of final triumph in God's perfected kingdom. While the personification of the Antichrist arose as a very early tradition – possibly as early as the 2nd century – this interpretation has persistently been challenged, and when John's epistles mention the term, the author is simply referring to opposition to Christ.

I believe that apocalyptic novels such as those of LaHaye and Jenkins, as well as the Islamic one which Dawoud mentions, are highly dangerous for several reasons. They present an erroneous and distorted view of the Bible and the Christian message. They have been justly criticised for their emphasis on terror, violence and war, and the amount of annihilation of entire cities in their apocalyptic speculation makes the 1945 destruction of Hiroshima and Nagasaki seem mild. Another similar series by Mel Odom (*Apocalypse Unleashed* and sequels) focuses on the armed forces, thus associating macho aggression with God's final plan for humanity. Trustworthy expressions of our three faiths, I believe, need to abandon irresponsible interpretations that rely on supernatural intervention (whether it is the coming of the Messiah, Christ's return on the clouds, or the return of Jesus and the Mahdi) and make us take our own share of responsibility in bringing about a better world, through negotiated settlements, compromise and mutual understanding.

Dawoud   Dan points out that for most Jews, especially in liberal and secular communities, the notion of an apocalypse has lost its importance. For many Muslims, however, there has been a swing in the opposite direction. The seeds of an apocalyptic message have been sown and have found fertile ground. In the space of only 50 years or so, a latent apocalyptic vision has been promoted and exploited to create a death cult which has drawn in many people and turned them from the joy of the world to a yearning for death and martyrdom and the achievement of the rewards graphically described in the Qur'an. While in absolute terms the apocalyptic groups remain a minority, they are destructive and dangerous, and elements of their ideas have leaked out into wider society, creating a kind of background noise to which people have become accustomed.

According to David Cook, the Islamist groups who espouse these ideologies line up a number of key targets as the main enemies of Islam who are to be defeated. The West is considered by many as synonymous with Christianity, although this is hardly the case. This simplistic device allows them to direct hostilities against the West on the basis that it is unacceptable for Christianity/the West, or indeed any other system, to have influence, as this would mean accepting their superiority. More specifically, the United States has been likened to the Antichrist, and US foreign policy as the way in which the Antichrist attempts to control the entire world. Although earlier apocalyptic literature makes little reference to Jews, in recent times a classical *hadith* is often quoted to support the anti-Israel stance:

> The Hour of Judgment will not arrive until the Muslims fight the Jews, and the Muslims will kill them until the Jew will hide behind rocks and trees, and the rock and the tree will say: O Muslim, O servant of God, there is a Jew behind me – come and kill him! (Cited in Cook, 2008:35)

(However, it may be noted that a similar *hadith* exists in which the enemy to be fought is the Turks.) Not least, Arab and Muslim leaders deemed to be corrupt or in league with the Western powers are just as much a threat to the pure Islam to which they aspire.

The inability of Muslims to prevail over the influence of these elements is perceived as failure, and as it is unacceptable for Islam to be so humiliated, then obviously they must not be doing enough to impose God's will. The fault cannot be God's, so it must be theirs. They must therefore fight harder, be ready to sacrifice more, punish those who disobey God, be more strictly observant (as they understand this) and put aside everything that is not directly related to doing God's will and bringing the world to Islam. Those who promote this vision have short-changed the recipients of their message by their selective rhetoric which chooses to ignore the spirit of God's will found in many parts of the Qur'an and Hadith that refer to peace, mercy, compassion, justice, equality and tolerance.

CHAPTER 14

What are the terrorists' motives?

Few readers – and certainly none of the authors – would be persuaded to join a terrorist organisation. So what makes its followers decide to join? Is there any way we can begin to understand their motives and purpose?

George   Not so long ago I read a media comment on Al-Qaeda which started, 'It all began with 9/11'. A moment's thought – although probably too much for the average tabloid reader – should indicate that 9/11 was not the beginning, and that Osama bin Laden did not decide to bomb the World Trade Center because he had nothing else to do. The event may have been decisive in world history but it had a background, which needs to be understood.

As I write this section, news is breaking of the terrorist attacks in Paris on 13 November 2015, when groups of terrorist attackers targeted the Stade de France, the Bataclan concert venue and three eating places in the city, almost simultaneously, indiscriminately shooting down around 130 innocent victims, and injuring around 350, before blowing themselves up. The obvious question is – why?

Because such actions are difficult – even impossible – to comprehend, they invite facile explanations. Some believe that those who are recruited to ISIS are 'brainwashed' – a process that changes personalities, causing recruits to abandon rational thinking in favour of blind obedience to their new-found leaders. Others have suggested that perpetrators of such violence are simply insane – an accusation that has sometimes been levelled against Adolf Hitler, whose fanatical hatred of the Jews went beyond the normal bounds of prejudice. And a few people have mentioned that Friday the 13th is supposedly an unlucky day.

Although there are no doubt elements of coercion and peer pressure, most academics reject 'brainwashing' theories, on the grounds that the concept is nebulous, and it is doubtful whether religious or political leaders can exercise such sway over recruits to elicit unquestioning conformity. Psychiatric disorder may underlie the actions of those individual gunmen who have entered schools and indiscriminately gunned down innocent children before ending their own lives. Their actions served no obvious purpose, apart from gaining themselves a short spell of media attention, which they would otherwise have been denied. Unlike the Nazis and terrorist organisations like ISIS and Al-Qaeda, these lone gunmen have not had any cause or any followers, and their social background has typically been seriously disturbed.

Where the perpetrators of extreme violence are part of a substantial organisation, it is more difficult to attribute brainwashing or mental illness to a wider group of people. In the case of ISIS, their goal is the setting up of a caliphate, starting in Iraq and Syria, and subsequently dominating the rest of the world. The fact that we can identify an ultimate goal does not mean, of course, either that such violence is justifiable or that it is efficacious in achieving the desired ends. Particularly in view of the world's overwhelming condemnation of their actions, it is difficult to see how ISIS can possibly believe that their actions are in any way effective. Unlike organisations like the IRA, ISIS and Al-Qaeda do not seem to be trying to terrorise their way to a negotiating table, and such a pointless terrorist attack makes their intended goal of establishing a world caliphate even less appealing. Who on earth would want to be a citizen in a regime that carried out beheadings, recruited child soldiers, engaged in sex trafficking, destroyed ancient cities and their priceless treasures, and prevented the practice of any alternative faith?

While it is possible to understand – although certainly not condone – their cause, what is less comprehensible is how such goals can be accomplished through these acts of indiscriminate violence.

Dawoud   George is absolutely right that 9/11 was not the beginning – it did not happen out of the blue. It was planned as an exercise in 'shock and awe' – to prove to the United States and the world that their actions in other parts of the globe would not always be without consequences. From the perspective of Al-Qaeda, it was a strike at the heart of the USA and the West, since what could be more symbolic of American and Western cultural and economic hegemony than the iconic twin towers of the World Trade Center? Regarding their other targets – the Pentagon and (we assume) the White House, one achieved and the other failed – both are symbolic of American military and political might.

Under the Ottoman Caliphate, the Islamic world had focus and prestige, but over two centuries or more prior to its eventual fall it traded away its economic strength in concessions given to European interests. Countries broke away from its power and ultimately it fell to the new European ideals of nationalism and secularism. The Ottomans had controlled the pilgrimage to Mecca for some 400 years until the rise of the Al-Saud family. With the discovery of oil in the Hejaz in the 1920s, the Saudis were cultivated by the USA and supported in power and obscene wealth. Elsewhere (for example and not in chronological order) following the Great War, Mesopotamia and the Levant were carved up by the Western powers and artificial borders were created and puppet regimes installed; Egypt and the Sudan were effectively controlled by Britain until 1922 and 1956, respectively; France, Spain and Italy had colonies in Algeria, Tunisia, Libya and Morocco; Britain had long colonised India and at different times held Malaysia and Burma as well as being deeply involved in Afghanistan; and the Dutch colonised Indonesia for more than three centuries. The collapse of British colonial rule led to the eventual partition of India and the creation of Pakistan and the problem of Kashmir. The British were highly influential in the Emirates and other parts of the Gulf, the Americans backed the Shah of Iran, and the former Soviet Union controlled a number of majority Muslim countries in the mid-20th century and went on to invade Afghanistan. The Balfour Declaration endorsed the British Government's support for the creation of a Jewish homeland in a land that did not belong to it, and the Western countries allowed the dispossession of hundreds of thousands of Palestinians after the Second World War and have continued to sponsor and protect the country that has kept them as refugees for more than 60 years and punished them disproportionately for every act of resistance.

The resentment has simmered for a hundred years; what many people see is a pattern of domination, exploitation of resources, manipulation and corruption of governments by Western countries and multinational businesses. The Muslim world has been broken and humiliated, and there is a perception that Muslim lives do not matter. Palestinians killed by Israel and Israelis outnumber Israelis killed by Palestinians by almost 10:1, but Israel is still the victim. Hundreds of thousands of Iraqi civilians including many children have been killed or have died of war and sanctions-related causes since the first Gulf War in 1990.

None of this justifies acts of terrorism, but it may go some way to explaining how it is possible for those who wish to radicalise young Muslims in the West to use selected rhetorical and graphic material to stir resentment and hatred.

Dan   George is right to question why ISIS has launched a murderous campaign against the West. Dawoud has given a political explanation for the rise of violent Islam. No doubt he is right that Muslims feel humiliated by their treatment in Western countries, and sense a profound loss of influence in modern times. Yet, this does not account for the fact that we are witnessing the emergence of a particular Islamic interpretation of history. Despite the claims by leading British politicians such as Theresa May (then Home Secretary, now Prime Minister) who said of the Paris attacks that they had nothing to do with Islam, as did United States President Obama, there is no doubt that radical jihadists are motivated by deeply held religious convictions. Their aim is to spread Islam through holy war using the tactics of shootings, stabbings, beheadings, disembowelling and human bomb attacks.

The quest to exonerate Islam from such atrocities is a misguided attempt to avoid lumping all Muslims together. Undoubtedly there are a wide range of Muslim believers – moderate as well as radical. But violent jihad is driven essentially by religious belief. The radical interpretation of Islam is based literally on the Qur'anic instructions to kill unbelievers as well as those who attack the faith. Such attitudes are endorsed throughout the Muslim world. Al-Azhar University in Cairo, for example, utilises curricular material which teaches that war against the infidels is an obligation of all intelligent, healthy, free and able men. Again, the 57-state Organisation of Islamic Cooperation which aims to promote Islamic solidarity excludes from its definition of terrorism armed struggle against foreign occupation, aggression, colonialism and hegemony.

Writing in *The Times* on 20 November 2015, Melanie Phillips notes that at present holy war is being waged by Muslims drawing on such a radical interpretation of the religion. The young Western Muslims they recruit are attracted by a mixture of social, political, psychological and religious factors. Some of these young people are involved with drugs and petty crime. Others are culturally and spiritually deracinated university students. But all are vulnerable to the jihadi message that gives their lives meaning and purpose by defending their people, Islam and Allah.

She writes:

> The incendiary impact is achieved through telling them the West is out to destroy the Islamic world. And what fries the brain is that this myth of victimhood arises from the Islamic inversion of reality. Islam is held to embody perfection because it is the word of God. Equality, freedom and justice are therefore to be found only under Islamic rule. So they can only exist in a theocracy, where there is in fact no equality, freedom or justice. Believers upholding such perfect Islamic precepts can never be at fault. So attacking infidels is never violence against the innocent but always justified defence.

Islam is thus an essential ingredient in the toxic mix of hatred and religious fervour. If we are to understand the nature of violent jihad, its essentially religious character must be acknowledged. We in the West are the victims of a holy war that seeks to destabilise our civilisation and destroy its values. Fortunately, there are Muslim modernisers who understand the nature of this problem and are seeking to reform the faith. It is their conviction that radical Islam must be identified and defeated. They need our support.

George   The Heidelberg Institute for International Conflict Research identifies several causes of war: ideology; desire for self-determination; a perceived need for national control; competition for resources; disputes about territory; and desire for independent control of part of one's own country, or for control of part of another country. Such causes may be related to desire for control over trade routes, historical disputes about land, and dwindling resources caused by growth in population or by climate change.

The Institute makes some mention of religion as a factor, but does not seem to regard it as a major one. The goal of a theocratically governed state that ISIS envisages could be construed as ideological rather than religious, although it has a clear religious dimension. Dan seems insistent that Islam should accept ownership of ISIS, but although the terrorists claim a Muslim identity they have been quite plainly disowned by Muslims worldwide. As I have previously argued, Dan's insistence is rather like saying that Christians should be held responsible for the activities of the Ku Klux Klan. No doubt Dawoud will comment further from his Islamic perspective, but – as I mentioned in my last exchange – the type of regime that ISIS wants to establish does not seem to reflect the principles of Islam, as I understand them.

We are discussing the causes of violence in this section, and there is a further aspect that deserves mention. By their very nature, terrorists can't wage war in the same way as governments. Governments finance military combat through taxation and, when it is judged necessary, conscription. Terrorist cells have to raise money by other, less legitimate, means. Monies collected through kidnapping and ransom demands are believed to have totalled US$20 million in 2014. Additionally, there are said to be wealthy individual donors, from whom US$40 million was received in 2013–2014. ISIS-controlled regions generate income through sales of oil, and arms are smuggled from Saudi Arabia, Iraq and Syria.

Because terrorist groups are relatively small, they would have little chance of military success in open face-to-face confrontation. This partly explains why their methods of combat have to be different: unexpected episodic acts of violence, which cannot readily be directed at key strategic targets but can only be perpetrated to induce terror. Much of the problem with terrorism is that those in command do not represent any official government, and in many cases it is not even clear who the leaders are. It is said, for example, that Al-Qaeda is a network of terrorists rather than a single unified organisation with a chain of leadership.

Violence too causes further violence. As armed conflict becomes a way of life, combatants can lose sight of the ultimate goal which appeared to legitimate the conflict, and the value of human life becomes progressively downgraded, with opponents simply being regarded as 'the enemy' rather than as human beings who have intrinsic worth. Hence no distinction is made between combatants and innocent bystanders, victims of kidnapping become commodities for fundraising, and women are recruited for the sexual gratification of male fighters. The terrorists appear to have lost track of how their acts of violence bring their desired Islamic state any closer, and whether their envisaged state is truly Islamic. Even in the extremely hypothetical event of the rest of humankind declaring that they had had enough of violence, and would accept government by the proposed caliphate, who would they negotiate with, and how would the world implement such a regime change? The so-called jihadists cannot win, but they can certainly cause much suffering and anxiety before they are finally defeated.

Dawoud   Again, and without contradicting what I said in the earlier part of this chapter, I have to agree with George that while groups such as ISIS and Al-Qaeda use selected material from the Qur'an and Hadith to justify their barbaric acts, they are not representative of the majority of Muslims worldwide. Dan believes that we should not attempt to exonerate Islam from the atrocities carried out in its name, but I fail to understand how blaming somewhere between 1.5 and 2 billion Muslims for the actions of a few tens of thousands of ISIS fighters will do anything but alienate the majority. We do not blame Judaism for the actions of armed Israeli settlers who attack and kill Palestinians in their own land and sometimes in their own homes, despite the fact that they base their claim to the land on scripture. We do not blame Christianity for apartheid, slavery, the Ku Klux Klan or the Lord's Resistance Army despite the fact that they are or were built on biblical foundations. We can only blame those people who are capable of conceiving of a God who would wish to see such violence, cruelty and destruction wreaked upon His own creation; those who falsely attribute their own murderous or exploitative agendas to a vengeful God; those who are so ignorant and arrogant as to imagine that they know the mind of God and are appointed to act in His name; those who think that God cares about what they wear and how they style their facial hair more than about their killing of other human beings.

What we must also not overlook is the fact that by several orders of magnitude the majority of the victims of ISIS and of other militant Islamic groups are other Muslims of different sectarian and ethnic backgrounds.

The agendas of different groups are certainly not all the same. In Iraq and Syria the underlying factors include centuries-old ethnic and sectarian divides that were previously kept in check by dictators and the apparatus of police states, while the attacks that have taken place in Europe have largely been carried out by 'home-grown' terrorists, many of whom were born and raised in Europe. For disaffected young men living as deprived minorities in sink communities with no aspiration and little opportunity, the notion of no longer being nothing but being part of something momentous, may be attractive, and it is these who are the most vulnerable to radicalisation.

France does not record religious affiliation in its census material so it is difficult to count the number of Muslims in the country, but estimates indicate that there may be as many as six million. We cannot hold six million people responsible for the actions of a handful of fanatics; if we allow terror to colour the relationships between communities of different faiths and none, and affect how we treat other people, if we lose sight of the fact that most Muslims want only the same as everyone else, to live with their families in peace and prosperity, then the terrorists will have succeeded in breaking down our societies – they will have won.

Dan Dawoud does not agree with my view about ISIS. There are several points I would make about his analysis:

(1) There is no doubt that the majority of Muslims are deeply troubled by the ideology of the so-called Islamic State. Recent sociological studies have demonstrated that the vast majority of Muslims living in the West deplore their views. Yet, it is a mistake to maintain, as did then Home Secretary Theresa May, that ISIS is not a Muslim organisation. This is a complete distortion of the facts. No one would wish to blame the Muslim community as a whole for the actions of ISIS. But if one wishes to understand the actions of radical jihadists, their religious motivation must be recognised, and their political theology needs to be placed into the context of the Islamic faith. From its inception, Islam has been spread by the sword, and the actions of modern jihadists carry on this tradition.

(2) As far as Judaism is concerned, it would be a similar mistake to regard the actions of religious Zionists as having nothing to do

with Judaism. This is true of secular Zionists who have distanced themselves from Jewish religious thought. But there are a sizeable number of Zionists today who seek to justify Israel's actions on the basis of the Hebrew Bible. In their view, God promised the land of Israel to Abraham and the Jewish nation. For this reason, these Zionists regard the Palestinians as aliens in the Holy Land despite the fact that they constituted the indigenous population prior to the creation of a Jewish state. It would be a mistake to blame all Jews for the actions of these religious Zionists, but it is an error to disassociate them from the Jewish tradition.

(3)   It is true that the majority of the victims of ISIS are Muslim. But this does not imply that Islam is not to blame for their suffering. The warring groups have different ideologies, but they all stem from the same source. As Muslims massacre each other, they believe they are carrying out the will of Allah.

(4)   No doubt many radical jihadists are European in origin and have experienced prejudice and discrimination. Dawoud is right that we should attempt to understand their frustration. At the same time their fanatical acts of violence should be condemned. In the face of the current threat, Muslims and non-Muslims must unite against this evil in our midst.

(5)   Dawoud is right that terror should not be allowed to colour the relationships between communities of different faiths. Yet, inevitably the murderous acts of violence perpetrated against the innocent in Paris, Brussels and elsewhere will generate Islamophobia. Regrettably newspapers such as *The Sun* have portrayed British Muslims in a negative light. Following the events that took place in Paris, for example, the front page of *The Sun* screamingly declared that a significant segment of the British Muslim population has sympathy for jihadists. This is hate-mongering of the worst kind. Yet, Islam is at the heart of jihadist ideology. It is undeniable that suicide bombers believe that they will be rewarded in heaven for their slaughter of infidels, and there are a significant number of religious Muslims who applaud their massacre of the innocent.

CHAPTER 15

Responses to terrorism

How should Jews, Christians and Muslims respond to terrorism? The use of force is one way, but is there any hope of peaceful reconciliation? Religions teach about forgiveness, but is this really a possible option?

Dawoud In Islam, forgiveness is first and foremost the privilege of God. In order to be forgiven, the wrongdoer must seek forgiveness from God and there are three requirements for this: firstly, the offence must be recognised and admitted before God; secondly, a commitment should be made not to repeat the offence; and thirdly, God's forgiveness should be asked for. Where the wrong is perpetrated against another person, the further condition for forgiveness from God is that the perpetrator acknowledge and seek pardon from the victim. With the exception of a very few individuals who have escaped the cult-like grip of groups such as ISIS, this is not a realistic prospect.

When we are in the middle of such a climate of terror it is hard to see how the world can be mended and how we can move forwards, even from our perspective in the West where we feel only a fraction of what is experienced by the people who live in the areas ravaged by civil war and inter-factional strife. In our lifetimes, however, we have witnessed reconciliations (or steps towards that goal) that we could not previously have imagined such as in the Irish peace process and in the fall of apartheid. What people most commonly seek is accountability and justice. In many instances, the actual perpetrators of terrorist crimes are killed by their own actions in suicide missions, or in battles with police or military forces, and while as individuals they are no longer a threat, they escape any form of judicial process. In some recent cases, targeted extra-judicial killings of known terrorists including Osama bin Laden and more recently the so-called 'Jihadi John' have also pre-empted any kind of trial for terrorism or war crimes that would hold them accountable before national or international courts. Following the Lockerbie bombing in 1988, despite the pain of losing his daughter Flora in the attack, Jim Swire fought for years for proper investigation and the establishment of an appropriate legal process to try those accused of the bombing and ultimately he challenged the conviction of one of those found guilty. He wanted those guilty of the crime to be held to account, and for him justice was more important than revenge, which so often only perpetuates the cycle of violence.

It is hard to imagine how the victims of terrorism or their families are ever able to forgive, or at least not to hate those who have destroyed their lives. Yet many times we have seen examples of individuals who have had the courage to free themselves from the burden of anger and the desire for revenge. Following the attacks in Paris on 13 November 2015, a young father whose wife was killed by the terrorists published an open letter to them and while he did not express forgiveness, he said:

> I will not give you the satisfaction of hating you. You want it, but to respond to hatred with anger would be to give in to the same ignorance that made you what you are. You would like me to be scared, for me to look at my fellow citizens with a suspicious eye, for me to sacrifice my liberty for my security. You have lost.

Dan Forgiving transgression is one of God's thirteen attributes in the Hebrew Bible (Exodus 34:6–7). In the sixth blessing of the *Amidah* prayer which is recited daily in the synagogue, God is addressed as 'The One who forgives abundantly'. Throughout Scripture God's forgiving nature is repeatedly asserted. Thus, for example, when the Israelites turned against the Lord and worshipped the golden calf, God heeded Moses' prayer and overcame his anger (Exodus 32:11–14). A central theme of the prophetic books is the need for repentance – an act made possible by God's capacity for forgiveness.

In the Middle Ages, the 12th century Jewish philosopher Moses Maimonides asserted that divine forgiveness is dependent on confession, repentance and the determination not to repeat the offence. In the Jewish faith these stages are highlighted and reflected in the liturgy. Each individual is to seek forgiveness from God and his neighbour. God is conceived as ready to forgive at the first sign of repentance, and human beings are urged to follow his example. However, it is understood that when one has committed an offence against another person, restitution is necessary and the offender must seek the injured party's forgiveness.

Underlying the Jewish view of forgiveness is the belief in God's mercy. According to Psalm 145:9, 'His compassion is over all that he has made'. Human beings too must adopt this quality. In the Jewish tradition, God is referred to as the Merciful One, yet he is continually forced to weigh the attribute of mercy against the attribute of justice. Thus, Jews also feel compelled to take into account the demands of justice in assessing the extent to which mercy should be shown. The relative priority of these concepts in rabbinic thought is illustrated in the Talmud where God is depicted as praying that his qualities of mercy and forgiveness should override the demand for strict justice.

These ideas about forgiveness parallel the Muslim tradition. Yet Christianity (as George will no doubt explain) has a fundamentally different orientation, and it is important that this distinction is stressed. In contrast with Judaism (and arguably Islam) – with its emphasis on individual repentance, restitution and reconciliation – the Church has understood forgiveness primarily as a gift, mediated through the life and death of Christ. Within the Jewish faith, the offender is to take the first step towards forgiveness through a change of heart. In Christianity, on the other hand, forgiveness is freely offered by God to sinners. God takes the initiative in drawing to him those who have fallen into sin, and the individual Christian is to forgive transgressors with the same loving spirit as God. In so doing, the way to repentance and reconciliation is opened through a vision of God's unconditional love. Jews, however, only feel the need to forgive those who repent, while Christians feel obliged to forgive their enemies unconditionally. What this means in effect is that Jews are under no obligation to forgive radical jihadists who seek to kill the innocent for the sake of Allah. Only if the conditions of repentance have been fulfilled can steps be taken to forgive the perpetrators of violent crimes against humanity.

George   I was once at an interfaith gathering where one member – I shall call him Mike – told the group that he had seen the Ulster Unionist Protestant leader Ian Paisley on television that morning and had said, 'I forgive you'.

This makes absolutely no sense to me. For something to count as an act of forgiveness, a number of conditions must be satisfied, and Dan and Dawoud have ably identified some of these. Dawoud mentions acknowledgement of wrong and seeking pardon from the victim; Dan identifies confession, repentance, determination to mend one's ways, and willingness to make restitution.

However, I think Dan is mistaken in his understanding of the Christian view of forgiveness and repentance. He correctly attributes to the Christian the notion that God has taken the initiative in forgiving humankind. Sin involves separation from God: in the Creation story Adam and Eve are separated from Paradise which God had created for them. Christ's incarnation signals that men and women, unable to make their own restitution, are met by God by a gracious act which makes forgiveness possible. Grace is freely available, but it can be accepted or rejected: traditional Christianity does not teach automatic universal forgiveness. Forgiveness is always associated with contrition and repentance, and a serious flaw in Mike's understanding was that there was no obvious change in Ian Paisley, not to mention the fact that Mike was not personally a victim of Paisley's fanaticism.

In the Gospel of Luke, Jesus says:

> If your brother or sister sins against you, rebuke them; and if they repent, forgive them. Even if they sin against you seven times in a day and seven times come back to you saying 'I repent', you must forgive them. (Luke 17:3–4)

Notice that, unlike Mike, Jesus does not mention forgiveness outside the context of repentance. However much I may try to feel positive towards someone who keeps on wronging me, feeling benign is not the same as being forgiving, and it is part of the meaning of the word 'forgiveness' that I cannot forgive until there are signs of contrition, and the wrongdoer at least makes a start in trying to behave differently. Jesus' teaching is that forgiveness is unlimited, not unconditional: if someone keeps wronging me, but shows genuine contrition each time, then I should keep on forgiving – up to seventy-seven times, in Matthew's version of Jesus' saying (Matthew 18:22).

Relating all this to terror and violence, I am not in a position to forgive ISIS or Al-Qaeda. I can certainly attempt to rid myself of hatred, try to understand why these organisations attract recruits and why they engage in their acts of violence. But the kind of indiscriminate forgiveness that Dan attributes to the ideal Christian is simply not feasible. The Christian faith also attaches importance to justice, to righteous anger and indeed to punishment, where appropriate. I am writing this the day after the British Parliament took the decision to bomb Syria as a response to recent jihadist acts. The Archbishop of Canterbury expressed his support for the air strikes. Many Christians, including myself, would disagree with him, but I don't think we can say he is not a Christian because he hasn't simply said 'I forgive you' to the terrorists.

Dawoud   George is of course quite right that forgiveness is meaningless unless it is sought or accepted. 'I seek forgiveness from God' is an expression used every day by Muslims who recognise omissions in their daily practice or in their mindfulness of God or who find themselves exposed to situations that they find morally or spiritually uncomfortable. For those radicals who are convinced that they are doing God's will and earning his favour, however, whether by fighting other Muslims in Syria and Iraq or launching attacks on Western targets, it does not even occur to them that they may need God's mercy and forgiveness for those acts. It hardly needs to be said that they certainly do not want nor do they even recognise ours.

While we may not forgive those who commit atrocities against other human beings, we should judge them as individuals and groups of individuals wholly accountable in this world and before God for their actions. We should not fall into the trap of blaming entire communities for the actions of a criminal minority. By doing so we play into the hands of those who seek to divide our societies and spread hatred and suspicion. If Western countries and societies start to treat their Muslim populations differently to others, they betray the very freedoms and standards of equality and justice that they stand for and they risk alienating entire communities. If we treat people with suspicion or make innocent citizens feel that we blame them for the actions of fanatics or suspect them of sympathising with them, we undermine their sense of belonging and inclusion. In extreme cases we may even push them into the arms of the radicals and fanatics. If we allow terrorists to make us change the way we behave towards other people, then we have already lost. Western democracies have long fought for codes of human rights, have separated the powers of government into the legislature, judiciary and executive, and have highly developed judicial systems with procedural regulations and standards of proof. Most importantly of all, we have the principle of 'innocent until proven guilty' and all those suspected of acts of terrorism whom we are able to apprehend should be subject to process of law in the same way as any other suspected criminals, for only by proper representation and fair trial can we guarantee safe convictions and appropriate punishment. This is what differentiates democracies from dictatorships, totalitarian regimes and self-appointed judges and executioners. What we cannot allow or support are abuses of these hard-won standards in the form of detention without trial, or even without charge, torture – or the condoning or ignoring of torture in other countries because it suits our purposes, or any form of discriminatory treatment on the basis of religion or ethnicity. Such things damage us as much as they hurt the people on whom they are inflicted. If we do not stand for human rights and equal treatment for everyone in society and before the law, then what are we fighting for?

Dan   Dawoud is right that we should not blame whole communities for the actions of some members. This, I fear, is what is currently happening to Muslims. The entire Muslim community is suspected of antipathy to Western values because of the rise of radical jihadism. But I am perplexed by George's exposition of the Christian view of forgiveness. His interpretation of the Christian attitude parallels my exposition of the Jewish view. But it has always been my understanding that they are fundamentally different.

In the New Testament the theme of repentance as a central feature of Jesus' ministry is introduced by John the Baptist (Mark 1:4). In Jesus' conception of God's Kingdom, forgiveness of sin was of main importance, and through his death forgiveness was made available for all. According to the New Testament view, God takes upon himself the act of reparation. In this way, the sinner can be restored to a true relationship with God. In Romans, Paul argues that the acceptance of this act of pure divine love is the moment of initiation into the Christian life (Romans 5:5–8).

God's love is thus wholly unconditional, free and unmerited, and as such it naturally calls out repentance from human beings. When Christians see God's reconciling love in Christ, their hearts are moved to repentance towards God and forgiveness towards others. Forgiveness is thus from God, and by God through Jesus' teaching ministry and death. Just as God forgives transgressors, so too must human beings forgive those who offend against them. In the Lord's Prayer, Christians are taught to pray: 'Forgive us our trespasses, as we forgive those who trespass against us'. In this way, the gift of forgiveness and repentance is available through the person and mission of Jesus Christ.

George is of course the expert in all this, and I am simply explaining how I have perceived the Christian view. My understanding is thus that Christians are obliged to forgive their enemies no matter what their attitudes. This I have always thought was the correct interpretation of the statement George referred to in Matthew. Here Jesus calls on his disciples to forgive and forgive and forgive. This, I thought, meant that sinners must be forgiven even if they show no contrition.

George, however, stresses the need for sinners to repent of their misdeeds as the first step towards forgiveness. Only by following in this path, he believes, is forgiveness possible. But I think this is not what Christianity really teaches. Rather, Christians are obliged to forgive sinners unconditionally. And it is such unconditionalness that is distinctive about Christian values. What this means in the context of violent jihad is that Christians are obliged to forgive terrorists no matter what their attitudes are. Radical jihadists and suicide bombers are to be forgiven even if they believe their violent acts are in accord with the will of Allah. Jews and Muslims, on the other hand, must not forgive murderers unless they themselves recognize the wrongness of their actions, repent of their sins and seek forgiveness from their victims or their victims' families.

George   The Lord's Prayer contains the line, 'Forgive us our trespasses, as we forgive those who trespass against us' (Luke 11:4). The petition implies a kind of mirroring between divine forgiveness and the human forgiveness that is expected of the Christian. The Christian tradition does not teach unconditional forgiveness. As I pointed out previously, the Bible invariably associates forgiveness with repentance, and the Christian tradition has maintained this association. Augustine is frequently quoted as saying 'God has promised forgiveness to your repentance'. Saint Thomas Aquinas taught that remorse, confession and satisfaction were needed in order to receive absolution from the priest during the sacrament of confession. The Council of Trent (1553) stated:

> There is no forgiveness without sorrow of soul, and forgiveness is always accompanied by God's grace; grace cannot coexist with sin; and, as a consequence, one sin cannot be forgiven while another remains for which there is no repentance. This is the clear teaching of the Bible.

The Protestant Reformers were less keen on outward acts of penance, such as fasting or saying the rosary, but nonetheless continued to associate forgiveness with repentance. The first of Martin Luther's 95 Theses was not about faith or grace, but about repentance: 'When our Lord and Master Jesus Christ said "Repent", he intended that the entire life of believers should be repentance'. John Calvin reaffirmed that forgiveness and repentance were interrelated, stating, 'no man can embrace the grace of the Gospel without betaking himself from the errors of his former life into the right path and making it his whole study to practise repentance' (*Institutes* 3,3,1). And in the Book of Common Prayer, absolution is not pronounced to all indiscriminately, but rather to 'all them that truly repent and unfeignedly believe his holy gospel'.

While Dan is correct to state that God has taken the initiative in offering forgiveness and grace, the word 'unconditional' is inappropriate. Grace and forgiveness are certainly available to all, but a human response is needed. It would be a very strange Christian who claimed to have received God's forgiveness, but intended to go on lying, stealing and committing adultery. Paul said, 'Shall we go on sinning, so that grace may increase? By no means!' (Romans 6:1–2). Divine forgiveness is not doled out to all indiscriminately!

At the very least certain conditions are needed for something to count as an act of forgiveness at all. This section is written a few days after presidential candidate Donald Trump declared that, if elected, he would ban all Muslims from entering the USA. Can I forgive him for that? I don't think so, since I have not been 'trespassed against'. Could the Muslim community forgive him? If Muslim leaders were to say, 'We forgive you', without any change having happened to Trump, I would be puzzled. What would they be doing? On the other hand, if Trump were to say that his remarks had been ill-chosen and that he regretted them, then we have the beginnings of scope for forgiveness. Forgiveness certainly involves attempting to remove hatred, resentment and desire for revenge, as well as a desire to understand why the wrongdoer acts as he or she does. These are qualities that Christians should cultivate, whether or not forgiveness is a possibility.

Could God forgive Trump? Christian teaching is certainly that all offences are offences against God, but I must leave God to decide who to forgive!

CHAPTER 16

The role of interfaith dialogue

The interfaith movement, which has gained momentum over the past few decades, offers a non-violent and constructive response to differences between our different faiths. Might interfaith activity offer a way forward in responding to terrorism and violence?

Dan   In the contemporary world, we are all faced with the threat of terrorism. How should our traditions respond? One course of action would be to retreat into tightly knit religious ghettos. Given our history, this is a serious temptation for Jewry. Through the centuries, we have faced persecution and murder. Our natural response has been to escape into the world of tradition. Yet today there is an opportunity – as never before – for Jews to reach out and learn from our gentile neighbours. Given the shift away from the absolutism of the past, modern Jews should be prepared to adopt an openness to other religious traditions.

Previously Jewish thinkers argued that Judaism contains God's fullest revelation to humankind. Today, however, in our religiously plural world, it is no longer possible to sustain such an exclusivist position. What is now required is a redefinition of theological exploration in view of the recognition that religious doctrines in all the world's faiths are ultimately human attempts to understand the nature of ultimate reality. In this light, we Jews must endeavour to learn from traditions other than Judaism. What this means in practice is that Jewish thinkers should be open to what the world's faiths have experienced and affirmed about the nature of divine reality, the phenomenon of religious experience, the nature of the self, the problem of the human condition, and the value of the world.

The dialogue that has taken place over the last fifteen chapters is arguably an example of such interfaith encounter. But there is a further step we should take in the light of the threat of terror and violence that we have been exploring. In contemporary society there is also the opportunity to pray together for peace, and to unite in worship and mourning for those who have died at the hands of radical jihadists and others. No longer should we feel constrained to stand apart from the services of other faith traditions. Interfaith worship should thus be at the forefront of our interfaith encounter.

But how is this to be done? The experience of interfaith worship and prayer is a relatively new religious activity. There are, I think, three major types of religious interfaith services which could be formulated as religions face the growing threat of violent action. Here I am drawing on the writing of Marcus Braybrooke, a major Christian expert on interfaith worship:

(1) Services of a particular religious community in which members of other faiths are invited as guests. On such occasions, it is usual to ask a representative of the visiting faith community to recite a suitable prayer or preach a sermon, but the liturgy remains the same.

(2) Interfaith gatherings of a serial nature. At such meetings representatives of each religion offer prayers or readings on a common theme. Those present constitute an audience listening to a liturgical anthology in which the distinctiveness of each religion is acknowledged, but everyone is free to participate as well.

(3) Interfaith gatherings with a shared order of service. In such situations all present are participants, and there is an overarching theme (Braybrooke; in Cohn-Sherbok, 1992:151).

In our global community religious communities face the challenge of living and praying together. As never before, we need to support one another in the face of the threat of terrorist attack. Understanding each other, uniting against terrorism, and comforting one another are crucial tasks for the future.

George Interfaith worship is all very well, but unfortunately I can't envisage many members of ISIS showing up! I'd like to mention something different.

I have recently returned from a pilgrimage to Israel, where we talked to a number of Palestinians. One group we met was called the Tent of Nations. Their leader lived on a portion of land in the West Bank, and possessed the title deeds which his family received from the Ottomans. Jewish settlers wanted the land, and when the owners refused to surrender it, they cut off water and power supplies. The Palestinian residents decided that they did not want to surrender as victims or to emigrate, but they wanted to avoid violence, so they decided on passive resistance. They continue to remain on the land, which they cultivate, and on which they run a small farm shop. Deprived of basic utilities, they use solar power for electricity and their own well for water, they collect rainwater in a cistern for irrigation, and they use a compost toilet.

Their dispute with the would-be settlers has been through legal channels, and they have received favourable court rulings, although at a practical level their situation remains unchanged. The site displays slogans such as 'Fight violence with love' and 'We refuse to be enemies', which sum up the community's philosophy. Members of the public can apply to attend celebrations, participate in workshops, and help the group's activities in planting and harvesting crops.

Our pilgrimage leader suggested that there were four Ps involved in building relationships, of which prayer was one. The other three were peace making, pilgrimage and pounds (financial contributions). Pilgrimage was what we were engaged in – visiting the land, talking to people, and learning about their situation at first hand. Making financial contributions is always easy for those of us who are better off, although the Tent of Nations is a business venture, selling quality products, which we were all too keen to purchase.

Peace making is no doubt the most difficult. How does one extinguish human greed, where would-be settlers try to acquire land that is not theirs, and engage in bullying tactics which would have persuaded most residents to leave? How does one make peace where there are conflicting claims about land ownership, particularly when such claims are backed up by quasi-religious justifications?

Interfaith worship is easy, especially when the weather is fine, and the venue is attractive and comfortable! Of course, there is merit in different faith groups affirming their commonality, and demonstrating their oneness. But getting together to share our devotional activities, sacred texts, and even affirming our communal concerns can be a very clean and sanitised way of persuading ourselves that we are making progress. We certainly need to meet each other, affirm our commonality, and share what we have in common, and I have no wish to distance myself from Dan's attempts at inter-religious dialogue in worship. However, we need to go beyond this. We need frankly to address the issues that have created conflict, explore potential solutions, and somehow extend our frontiers to bring in those who are inimical to peace making. Interfaith dialogue has largely been about being nice to each other. This is certainly a start, and much preferable to being hostile! But the interfaith movement needs to move beyond this, and be able to discuss frankly and act upon the serious problems that divide members of different faiths. That is the real challenge.

Dawoud   Any kind of dialogue between people of different faiths, cultures and ethnicities is, of course, a positive thing, but as George has indicated, in reality this has only limited impact when those who are involved are the people who are already persuaded of the necessity of mutual understanding and peaceful coexistence.

For obvious reasons, we have focused in this discussion on what we too readily refer to as Islamic terrorism, which has dominated the news on a daily basis for the last few years. Islamist terrorists, or those criminals who self-identify as Muslims and believe themselves to be doing God's will whilst murdering and maiming the innocent, have no interest in making peace on a basis of mutual acceptance and respect. No interfaith dialogue could have reached those who carried out the violent attacks in Paris in November 2015 or in California in December 2015, and it would certainly have no effect whatsoever on the Islamic State group and others committing atrocities in Iraq, Syria and other parts of the region. The absolutism of the perpetrators of such violence and the totalitarian ideology of the movement out of which they have emerged make them impervious to reason or threat and therefore more terrifying than any normal enemy. What possible negotiation can there be with someone who believes they stand for an absolute right and whose dearest longing is to die for their cause?

It is difficult not to despair of any kind of just and lasting solution to the turmoil that has beset the Middle East since the first Gulf War, the roots of which go back much further. A toxic cloud of backward and reactionary ideology has spread and infiltrated far beyond its source and threatens Muslim communities everywhere; it has undone the work of generations of reformers and propagated a dismal monoculture in the place of centuries of diversity and progress. The Islamist war on women has disabled a substantial section of the population. Those who have not been duped into believing that by giving up so many of the rights hard-won by their mothers and grandmothers that they are somehow newly empowered in their identity, are often silent out of fear, both for themselves and for their families. Many Muslims are too ill-informed about their own faith to have the confidence to stand against the intimidation of the Islamist rhetoric, or simply too afraid of the consequences of being accused of blasphemy, heresy or apostasy if they challenge hard-line opinions. This is understandable when many of the most authoritative Islamic scholars and institutions have failed adequately to condemn the Islamist distortions of Islamic faith and culture that are used to justify atrocities.

Within our own communities perhaps the most important thing that we can do is to ensure that the values that are important to us are not compromised. This means that we must not tolerate any undermining of the principles of absolute equality out of misguided sensitivity to religion or culture, and at the same time we must not accept any discrimination or persecution of people because they happen to be of the same faith as the terrorists. If we allow the terrorists to change our behaviour and standards, then they will have succeeded.

Dan Dawoud is right that there seems to be no way for both Christians and Jews to reach out to fundamentalist Muslims who are intent on carrying out murderous acts of terror. They are impervious as well to those Muslims who call on them to embrace those principles of tolerance and cooperation which are deeply embedded within the Islamic tradition. Interfaith relations in this context are impossible. But this is not so in other areas of religious life. I have already mentioned interfaith prayer as a meeting point for believers from different faith communities. There is a long history of interfaith encounter stretching back through the centuries which should serve as a basis for understanding and reconciliation.

Yet George is right that interfaith relations must not obscure the need to face up to critical problems which separate our religious communities. Here I want to focus on the conflict between the Palestinians and the Israelis. In a previous book (*The Palestine-Israeli Conflict*) Dawoud and I explored the nature of this struggle. Throughout Dawoud pressed the Palestinian case, arguing that from the early 20th century until today Israel has been the aggressor in this conflict and that Israel is guilty of numerous crimes against the Palestinian people. By contrast, I stressed that throughout this conflict Palestinians have been unable to reach any form of compromise with Jewish immigrants who settled on the land. Rather they have unleashed a campaign of terror and violence against the Jewish nation, seeking to drive Israelis into the sea. What is clear from our discussion is that both Israelis and Palestinians have profoundly suffered in this ongoing conflict. This is the tragedy of the Holy Land. Neither people has a monopoly on human anguish. Regrettably it is difficult, if not impossible, for Palestinians to acknowledge the suffering of Israelis, and for Israelis to accept that their government has been responsible for the deep despair of the Palestinians, particularly those in refugee camps. This lack of empathy has made fruitful relations between Jews and Muslims impossible. Arguably what is needed is for both sides to come to terms with the evils they have inflicted on each other. From long experience with the Jewish community, I know that for many Jews this would be unacceptable, nothing less than a moral and religious capitulation. But it is precisely such a step which is required if there is eventually to be a just solution to the Middle East problem.

In the meantime, there currently exist groups and individuals who are seeking to pave the way to greater cooperation and understanding. A prime example of such efforts is the creation of the West–Eastern Divan Orchestra by the Israeli conductor Daniel Berenboim and the late Palestinian academic, Edward Said. The orchestra was created in 1999 and is based in Seville, Spain. It consists of musicians from countries in the Middle East, of Egyptian, Iranian, Israeli, Jordanian, Lebanese, Palestinian, Syrian and Spanish backgrounds. In the words of Daniel Berenboim:

> The Divan was conceived as a project against ignorance. A project against the fact that it is absolutely essential for people to get to know one another, to understand what the other thinks and feels,

without necessarily agreeing with it. I'm not trying to convert the Arab members of the Divan to the Israeli point of view, and [I'm] not trying to convert the Israelis to the Arab point of view. But I want to . . . create a platform where the two sides can disagree and not resort to knives. (Wikipedia, 2016b)

George Whether or not interfaith worship is the way forward, we would all do well to take heed of the World Council of Churches' Guidelines on Dialogue with People of Living Faiths and Ideologies which was agreed in Chiang Mai in 1977, published in 1979, and can be found on the WCC website. Agreed statements are often dry and uninteresting, but this one is an exception.

The British Council of Churches (now Churches Together in Britain and Ireland) has summarised the WCC's statement in four broad principles, which are expanded in a number of further guidelines (World Council of Churches, 1979; British Council of Churches, 1981). These are:

(1) 'Dialogue begins when people meet each other.' When I was an undergraduate, the world's religions were taught through lectures and books. It was much later that I came into contact with actual people, which enabled me to recognise that religious belief was not simply about ideas, but about human life. Followers of religions do not always read the textbooks, and one can find large differences between textbook religion and lived religion.

(2) 'Dialogue depends upon mutual understanding and mutual trust.' Mutual understanding occurs when partners in dialogue can explain their faith to each other. One of the explanatory guidelines states, 'Adherents of other faiths must be allowed to define themselves in their own terms'. This highlights the importance of listening to and accepting the believer's authentic account, rather than relying on media portrayals and popular misconceptions. A Muslim's insistence that *jihad* means inner striving rather than holy war is important testimony to the way those who belong to the Islamic faith understand themselves, and is much to be preferred to the media portrayals of Muslims as warmongers or terrorists.

(3) 'Dialogue makes it possible to share in service to the community.'
Whether or not members of different faiths can pray and worship
together, there are matters on which differences of faith need not
divide us, and there have been numerous examples of common
endeavours, ranging from members of different faiths communally
planting trees in a locality, to collectively protesting against
discriminatory legislation. One very important act of communal
service can be accomplished where media publicity is given to an
event which seemingly tells against one religion. In the wake of
the *Charlie Hebdo* massacre and the Paris attacks, it was important
for all faiths to emphasise that these were not actions sanctioned
by Islam, and that all three faiths dissociated themselves from this
kind of violence.

(4) 'Dialogue becomes the medium of authentic witness.' One of the
worries about interfaith dialogue has been that it might be used as
a subtle form of Christian evangelism after the heyday of Christian
mission. This is certainly not the intention. Authentic witness is not
simply the prerogative of Christians, but of all faiths who engage
in dialogue. The WCC guidelines add that 'Dialogue with people
of other faiths means discovering they have insights into truth
to share with us'. One Christian colleague has coined the phrase
'holy envy', recognising the possibility that I may see something in
another faith my own neglects, and that I might positively like to
take on board.

Dialogue need not exclude criticism and, as I have previously mentioned,
I believe there is scope in the interfaith agenda for airing our differences
in a friendly but frank manner, as the three authors have attempted to
do in this book. Although we can discuss the details of what interfaith
activity might involve, there is certainly a need to bring people of
different faiths together in an atmosphere of friendship, tolerance and
mutual understanding.

Dawoud   At the risk of deviating from the topic, I have to take issue with Dan
in relation to some of the points he raises. I do not want to discuss the
Palestine–Israel issue here at any length as we have debated and will no
doubt continue to debate it in other forums. There are, however, points
that are relevant to the issue of terror and violence both on a global and

a specific level, and amongst the most significant and relevant of these here and in so many other conflicts and revolutions are inequality and injustice.

It is disingenuous to suggest, as the pro-Israel lobby would have it, that on any level the hostile actions of Palestinians and Israelis towards each other are comparable, or that the Palestinian threat to Israel is greater than the Israeli threat to Palestinians. There is an immense power divide between the two. Israel is one of the most highly armed states in the world and holds the power of life and death over the people on whose land it was built and who remain stateless in Gaza and the West Bank. Israel controls the entire territory militarily and administratively; it can shut off power and water and restrict supply of foodstuffs and other goods to Palestinians in Gaza, launch the full force of a highly trained army with state-of-the-art equipment against civilian communities and carry out collective punishments on its own terms. If we compare the casualty statistics amongst Palestinians and Israelis, including those relating to the deaths and injuries of children, we find that they are of a different order of magnitude. The Israeli state operates an institutionalised policy of ethnic and religious discrimination which would not be acceptable in any other context. There is no equality of opportunity either on a personal or a community level for Palestinians whose lives are somehow deemed less valuable than those of Israelis and whose existence as a people is effectively less important than that of Israel. While I condemn violence of all kinds, it is difficult to imagine how there can ever be peace without justice and equality, and it is even more difficult to imagine how justice and equality for the Palestinians will ever be achieved.

Both Dan and George have emphasised the importance of dialogue and cooperative action between faith groups, and of course this is essential. It is equally important, however, and potentially more effective, for those who seek peace to engage their own faith groups in debate, to have the courage to challenge ignorance and bigotry in their own communities, to refuse to allow the argument to be reduced to the lowest common denominator, and to spread information and education about the real messages of their faiths as they understand them. We have to stand for freedom of speech both amongst and between our faith groups. As George points out, nothing and no-one should be above criticism. If an opinion is not aired, it cannot be challenged; like an accused person in the dock, if an opinion has valid representation then if it is 'innocent' it will be vindicated, but if it is proved 'guilty' then it cannot be claimed that it was due to inadequate representation or unfair process.

In all of our faiths there are messages of peace and injunctions to treat others as we would wish to be treated, and I think we have to prove this to ourselves before we attempt to convince others.

CHAPTER 17

Conclusions

In this concluding chapter the three authors offer some final reflections on the discussion.

Dan We are now at an end to this exploration of terror, war and violence. Throughout this discussion, I believe, there have emerged two varying perspectives. Repeatedly George and Dawoud have stressed that violent action in its varying forms has fundamentally been the result of human motivation rather than the outcome of religious ideals and principles. While recognising that both Christianity and Islam have been responsible for unspeakable horrors, they have stressed that this is a human rather than religious phenomenon. In both faith traditions, they argue, the cardinal virtues of love, benevolence and peace have been overwhelmed by human hatred. There is thus an underlying tension between the moral tenets of these two religious traditions and human intentions and motivation.

Such a defence of Christianity and Islam is fundamentally at odds with critics of religion who maintain that religion itself has been responsible for horrendous evil in both the past and the present. In our trialogue I have largely taken this position. In my view our three faiths are culpable for horrendous crimes against humanity. As a world power this has been particularly true of Christianity – Christian history is awash with blood. Regarding its relationship with Judaism, it has perpetuated antisemitic attitudes for nearly 2,000 years. In the past Islam spread its message by the sword and in the modern period jihadists are carrying on this tradition of hatred and violence. Because Jews have been a minority people living in foreign lands, they previously lacked the power to overwhelm their neighbours. But today in Israel, Jews are engaged in an ongoing struggle against those Palestinians in their midst and others in the Occupied Territories. This has resulted in untold human suffering.

It is vital that we recognise that in the past religion itself, not simply human beings, has been responsible for persecution, suffering and death, and that in the modern world – in various ways – it continues its violent campaign against the innocent. This, of course, is not the whole story. As Dawoud and George have pointed out, our three faiths also proclaim the highest standards of compassion and justice. In the Jewish tradition, the prophets of ancient Israel, who spoke in God's name, symbolise such ideals. Jesus' message of love in the New Testament is paramount. The Qur'an is a storehouse of moral principles. Dawoud and George are right to highlight these ideals. But they are only one dimension of a more complex picture.

What then is the path forward? We must, I believe, acknowledge the discrepant character of religious faith in the great monotheistic traditions. Its high principles are embedded in historical contexts dripping with blood. From the massacre of the Canaanites in ancient Israel to the recent slaughter by jihadists in Paris, the faithful have been determined to champion their cause by violent means. Such slaughter is not an aberration of religion – instead it is deeply embedded in the religious tradition itself. Faith then contains within itself the seeds of human destruction. Only by acknowledging this danger, and understanding its root causes, can we counter this tendency to terror, violence and war.

Dawoud   In his famous song 'Imagine' (1971), John Lennon invited us to envisage a world without countries, without causes to die for and without religion – which was his formula for living in peace. However, I cannot agree with Dan that religion is the root cause or source of violence. I believe it is human nature; survival, competition for land and resources, power struggles, greed, ambition and vested interests are dressed up in religion. If it were not for religion, I have no doubt that human beings would build their disputes and wars around something else.

Hostility between communities is not a new phenomenon. We are a tribal species; tribalism is as old as humanity itself and has changed and taken many forms over the centuries. However much we may think of ourselves as individuals, our security and prosperity are ultimately bound up with the survival of the group to which we belong. For many, this is embodied in belonging to a faith community – a religion or one of many denominations of a single religion – which is often indistinguishable from a regional, ethnic or clan community.

If we want to prevent terrorism and violence in the name of religion we have to address the underlying issues: injustice, inequality, tyranny, corruption, poverty, exploitation and lack of prospects and hope for a prosperous future. Where one community identifies a ruler or government, or another community, as the cause of its suffering or a threat to its existence, it may not take much to convince them that their enemies are heretics, blasphemers, apostates or infidels and not just ordinary self-interested dictators, worldly rivals or competitors for resources. By the same token, those who do not feel that they belong or have an interest or stake in the society around them may seek a place, an identity and security elsewhere. In our own society at least, we have to ensure that there is equal opportunity for all and we have to find ways especially to help those who do not find the answers they need. Religion is rarely the sole motivation in any hostilities but it is the most powerful rallying cry. There is no reason or argument against those who believe they are doing the will of God, or those who seek to control their communities by claiming to possess divine truth.

In the Qur'an, Surat al-Hujurat, God says: 'O mankind, indeed We have created you from male and female and made you peoples and tribes that you may know one another' (49:13). If we are truly to know one another, we have to recognize and acknowledge that we have differences, but we are not 'other'. There is value and delight in diversity, but we are all equal in our humanity.

George I think our discussion has highlighted the complexity of these problems, and readers should not expect us to provide a remedy to solve the world's difficulties. I have argued that religion is not a 'thing' that can be isolated from other aspects of life, such as politics, technology and ideology. To suggest that religion is responsible for violence, terror and war is as sensible as suggesting that science and technology are the culprits. While there are links between some religious ideas and violence, Dan is right to point to this gap between the ideal and the real.

If only we could fully implement our religions' ideals of love, justice and peace!

At this point in the discussion we should be summing up rather than introducing new ideas, but I should like to add one new thought to our dialogue. Throughout their history religions have been preoccupied with the end times, proclaiming an imminent winding up of human affairs. As I suggested earlier, this may cause human beings to see little point in caring for the planet and even to think that we should give Armageddon a helping hand!

We think human life is fragile and fear that life on earth could be destroyed in a variety of ways – massive volcanic eruption, asteroids, global warming or global freezing, or incurable plagues, and of course human beings could totally destroy themselves with nuclear weapons. However, none of these outcomes are certain, and they would not necessarily eliminate all human life. Barring supernatural intervention, scientists reckon that human life on earth could be sustainable for something like 7.79 billion years. Maybe the end is not nigh after all, and maybe religions should place humankind at the beginning of their spiritual journey on earth, rather than near the end. Perhaps we are only beginning to learn how to show the virtues of love, justice and peace.

Christian fundamentalists have accepted a literal belief in Christ's imminent return on the clouds of heaven to wind up a chaotic world that humans cannot restore by their own efforts. However, numerous Christian scholars have pointed out the obvious fact that over two millennia have elapsed since these expectations began. Saint Augustine, writing in the 5th century, was possibly the first to acknowledge that the Church had a history, and was not just a fleeting entity awaiting a supernatural winding up of human affairs. In common with many present-day biblical scholars, I believe we need to recognise that many biblical ideas are wrapped up in 1st century imagery that need not be taken literally. While fundamentalists highlight the eschatological expectations in Jesus' parables, such as the absentee landlord whose stewards are entrusted with his estate until he returns (Mark 12:1–12; Matthew 24:45–51), other Christians have focused on the stewardship that these parables enjoin. Whatever kind of future God has planned for humankind, we must exercise responsibility in the meantime, and not destroy the planet through greed, negligence or violence.

We still have a long way to go to be able to live in harmony, relinquishing centuries of past scores to settle, distrust and hatred, desire for vengeance, and beliefs in inalienable territorial rights. In theory, our three respective faiths are agreed in teaching the ideals of love, justice and peace. If the earth has a further 7.79 billion years to go, we are just starting out on a long journey towards a peaceful and harmonious society. Let us hope it will not take that amount of time to learn to live together.

Glossary

Ahmadiyya   Islamic sect, founded in the late 19th century in the Punjab.

Al-Qaeda   Terrorist group founded by Osama bin Laden and others in 1988, in the wake of the Soviet invasion of Afghanistan.

apocalypse   Literally, the unveiling of something hidden. Because of the content of the Books of Daniel and Revelation, the term has come to be associated with the end times and the tribulations associated with them.

Baha'i   A sect derived from Islam, founded in the 19th century by Bahá'u'lláh (Mírzá Ḥusayn-`Alí Núrí), who is believed to be the prophet for the present age, coming after Jesus and Muhammad.

caliphate   An area with a caliph as ruling authority. A caliph is someone who is judged to be a successor of Muhammad.

Conservative Judaism   Emerged in the 19th century as a reaction to both Orthodoxy and Reform Judaism. It seeks to occupy a middle position between these two movements.

covenant   Biblical term for a legal agreement between two parties, especially between God and his people (Jews, and later Christians).

Daesh   Ad-Dawla Al-Islamiyya fi'l-Iraq wa'sh-Sham (Islamic State of Iraq and Greater Syria/Levant). This name is sometimes favoured by Muslims since the reference to Islam is less obvious.

eschatology   Teachings about the end times.

Essenes   Monastic Jewish sect in Palestine at the end of the Second Temple period.

fundamentalism   Originally an early 20th century conservative Christian school of thought that entailed belief in the inerrancy of the Bible. The term has now come to denote extremist forms of various religions.

Hadith   The collected reports of the words, deeds and tacit acceptance of the Prophet Muhammad.

Hasidim   A religious movement founded by the Baal Shem Tov in the 18th century in Eastern Europe. Its followers are referred to as Hasidim. It is a strictly Orthodox sect stressing spirituality and mysticism.

IRA   Irish Republican Army, a paramilitary organisation committed to achieving the independence of all Ireland.

Irgun   A Zionist paramilitary organisation that operated in Mandate Palestine between 1931 and 1948.

ISIS   Islamic State of Iraq and Syria.

jihad   Popularly translated as 'holy war'. However, the term also means 'striving', which entails combatting the forces of evil within oneself, as well as outside.

Ka'aba   Islam's most holy shrine, at Al-Masjid al-Haram, in Mecca, and the focal point of the Hajj. It is believed to have been built by Abraham.

Maimonides   Famous Jewish scholar, living in the 12th century.

Midrash   Rabbinical interpretation of Scripture. There are many different versions of midrashim.

Mishnah   The first major written redaction of the Jewish oral traditions known as the 'Oral Torah'. It is the first major work of rabbinic literature.

Orthodox Judaism Traditional Jewish movement stressing the divine origin of the Written and Oral Law that insists on strict adherence to the Code of Jewish Law.

Pharisees A religious sect of the Second Temple period.

Reform Judaism Emerged in the early part of the 19th century. It is a movement designed to modernise Jewish life and thought.

Sadducees First century conservative Jewish school of thought, focused on the Jerusalem Temple and its rites.

Sanhedrin Jewish court in biblical times.

Shari'a Islamic law, derived from the Qur'an and the Hadith.

Shi'a (adj. Shi'i) Abbreviation of Shi'at 'Ali, the party of Ali. Division of Islam which regards Ali (632–661) – Muhammad's son-in-law – as the true successor of Muhammad. It is particularly prevalent in Iran, and is espoused by around 10% of all Muslims.

Sinn Féin Irish political party, aiming to achieve the independence of all Ireland.

Stern Gang A Zionist paramilitary organisation founded by Avraham Stern in Mandate Palestine.

Sunna (adj. Sunni) The custom or tradition of the Prophet which is the model for the behaviour of Muslims. Abbreviation of Ahl as-Sunna – the people of the tradition of the Prophet. Division of Islam which acknowledges Umar, Uthman and Abu Bakr as Muhammad's successors, and which is followed by the majority of Muslims worldwide.

Talmud The Palestinian and Babylonian Talmud refers to two collections of records of Jewish law by rabbinic sages from c.200–c.500.

Tawrat Islamic term for the Jewish Torah, which Muslims hold to have been sent down from heaven to Moses, but which became distorted through time.

Torah The first five books of Jewish scripture (Genesis, Exodus, Leviticus, Numbers, Deuteronomy), also referred to as the Law or the Pentateuch.

Zionism Initiated by Theodor Herzl, Jewish Zionism advocated a return of the Jews to Palestine. Jewish Zionism is secular, in contrast to Christian Zionism, which views the return of the Jews as a fulfilment of biblical prophecy, as a prelude to Christ's return.

Further reading

Christianity

Bruyneel, Sally and Padgett, Alan G. (2003). *Introducing Christianity.* Maryknoll, NY: Orbis.

Chryssides, George D. (2010). *Christianity Today.* London: Continuum.

Chryssides, George D. and Wilkins, Margaret Z. (2011). *Christians in the Twenty-first Century.* Sheffield, UK: Equinox.

Kim, Sebastian and Kim, Kirsteen (2008). *Christianity as a World Religion.* London: Continuum.

Woodhead, Linda (2004). *Christianity: A Very Short Introduction.* Oxford: Oxford University Press.

Islam

Esposito, John (2011). *What Everyone Needs to Know About Islam.* New York: Oxford University Press.

Esposito, John and Mogahed, Dalia (2008). *Who Speaks for Islam? What a Billion Muslims Really Think.* New York: Gallup Press.

Geaves, Ron (2011). *Islam Today.* London: Continuum.

Gilliat-Ray, Sophie (2010). *Muslims in Britain.* Cambridge: Cambridge University Press.

Hourani, Albert (1991). *Islam in European Thought.* Cambridge: Cambridge University Press.

Lings, Martin (1983). *Muhammad: His Life Based on the Earliest Sources.* Cambridge: Islamic Texts Society.

Ruthven, Malise (2012). *Islam: A Very Short Introduction.* Oxford: Oxford University Press.

Judaism

Blech, Benjamin (2003). *The Complete Idiot's Guide to Judaism.* London: Alpha.

Cohn-Sherbok, Dan (2003). *Judaism: History, Belief and Practice.* London: Routledge.

Cohn-Sherbok, Dan (2010). *Judaism Today.* London: Continuum.

de Lange, Nicholas (2010). *An Introduction to Judaism.* Cambridge: Cambridge University Press.

Hoffman, C. M. (2010). *Judaism.* London: Teach Yourself.

Lehman, Oliver (2011). *Judaism: An Introduction.* London: I. B. Tauris.

Solomon, Norman (2000). *Judaism: A Very Short Introduction.* Oxford: Oxford University Press.

Interfaith dialogue

Braybrooke, Marcus (1992). *Pilgrimage of Hope: One Hundred Years of Global Interfaith Dialogue.* London: SCM.

Braybrooke, Marcus (1996). *A Wider Vision: A History of the World Congress of Faiths 1936-1996.* Oxford: Oneworld.

British Council of Churches (1983). *Can We Pray Together? Guidelines on Worship in a Multi-Faith Society.* London: British Council of Churches.

El-Alami, Dawoud, Cohn-Sherbok, Dan and Chryssides, George D. (2014). *Why Can't They Get Along?* Oxford: Lion Hudson.

Küng, Hans and Kuschel, Karl-Josef (eds.) (1993). *A Global Ethic: The Declaration of the Parliament of the World's Religions.* London: SCM.

Smock, David (2002). *Interfaith Dialogue and Peacebuilding.* Washington, DC: United States Institute of Peace Press.

Politics and Middle Eastern affairs

Al-Yaqoubi, [Shaykh] Muhammad (2015). *Refuting ISIS: A Rebuttal of Its Religious and Ideological Foundations.* Kirklees, UK: Sacred Knowledge Trust.

Cockburn, Patrick (2015). *The Rise of Islamic State: ISIS and the Rise of the New Sunni Revolution.* London and New York: Verso.

Husain, Ed (2007). *The Islamist: Why I Joined Radical Islam in Britain, What I Saw Inside and Why I Left.* London: Penguin.

Nesser, Petter (2015). *Islamist Terrorism in Europe.* Oxford: Oxford University Press.

Osman, Tarek (2016). *Islamism: What It Means for the Middle East and the World.* New Haven and London: Yale University Press.

Payne, Ronald (1991). *Mossad: Israel's Most Secret Service.* London: Corgi.

Sacks, Jonathan (2015). *Not in God's Name: Confronting Religious Violence.* London: Hodder and Stoughton.

Works cited

Allport, Gordon (1954/1989). *The Nature of Prejudice*. London: Addison-Wesley.

Armstrong, Karen (2015). *Fields of Blood: Religion and the History of Violence*. London: Vintage.

Augustine (1957). *The City of God* (transl. John Healey). 2 vols. London: Dent.

Avineri, Shlomo (1981/1984). *The Making of Modern Zionism: The Intellectual Origins of the Jewish State*. London: Weidenfeld and Nicolson.

BBC News Channel (2004). Atkinson's religious hate worry. 7 December 2004. Accessible online at http://news.bbc.co.uk/1/hi/uk_politics/4073997.stm (accessed 8 December 2004).

British Council of Churches (1981). *Relations with People of Other Faiths: Guidelines on Dialogue in Britain*. London: British Council of Churches.

Calvin, John (1559/1962). *Institutes of the Christian Religion*. 2 vols. London: James Clarke.

Central Intelligence Agency (2015). *The World Factbook*. Accessible online at https://www.cia.gov/library/publications/resources/the-world-factbook/geos/xx.html (accessed 28 June 2015).

Church of England (1662/1968). *The Book of Common Prayer*. Glasgow: Collins.

Cohn-Sherbok, Dan (1992). *Many Mansions*. London: Bellew.

Cohn-Sherbok, Dan (1997). *The Crucified Jew: Twenty Centuries of Christian Antisemitism*. Grand Rapids, MI: Eerdmans.

Cohn-Sherbok, Dan (2002). *Antisemitism: A History*. Stroud: Sutton.

Cohn-Sherbok, Dan (2006). *The Paradox of Anti-Semitism*. London: Continuum.

Cohn-Sherbok, Dan and El-Alami, Dawoud (2001). *The Palestine-Israeli Conflict*. Oxford: Oneworld.

Cook, David (2008). *Contemporary Muslim Apocalyptic Literature*. Syracuse, NY: Syracuse University Press.

Dawkins, Richard (2007). *The God Delusion*. London: Black Swan.

El-Alami, Dawoud, Cohn-Sherbok, Dan and Chryssides, George D. (2014). *Why Can't They Get Along?* Oxford: Lion Hudson.

The Guardian. (2007). What Muslim journalists think about the UK media. 19 November 2007. Accessible online at http://www.theguardian.com/media/

organgrinder/2007/nov/19/howmuslimjournalistsfeelab (accessed 24 January 2016).

Heidelberg Institute for International Conflict Research (2015). *Conflict Barometer*. Accessible online at http://www.hiik.de/en/konfliktbarometer/pdf/ConflictBarometer_2014.pdf (accessed 24 January 2016).

Herzl, Theodor (1896) (transl. Sylvie D'Avigdor). *The Jewish State*. London: David Nutt.

International Terrorism and Security Research. *Terrorism Research*. Accessible online at www.terrorism-research.com (accessed 29 March 2016).

Jacobs, Louis (1995). *The Jewish Religion: A Companion*. Oxford: Oxford University Press.

LaHaye, Tim and Jenkins, Jerry B. (1995). *Left Behind: A Novel of the Earth's Last Days*. Wheaton, IL: Tyndale House.

Leveson, L. J. (2012). *An Inquiry into the Culture, Practices and Ethics of the Press*. London: The Stationery Office. Accessible online at https://www.gov.uk/government/uploads/system/uploads/attachment_data/file/229039/0779.pdf (accessed 29 March 2016).

Luther, Martin (1543). *The Jews and Their Lies*. Accessible online at https://www.jewishvirtuallibrary.org/jsource/anti-semitism/Luther_on_Jews.html (accessed 24 January 2016).

Odom, Mel (2008). *Apocalypse Unleashed*. Carol Stream, IL: Tyndale House.

Open Doors (2015). *World Watch Country Profiles*. Accessible online at www.opendoorsuk.org/persecution/country_profiles.php (accessed 23 August 2015).

Phillips, Charles and Axelrod, Alan (2008). *Encyclopaedia of Wars*. Los Angeles: Facts on File.

Phillips, Melanie (2015). The false victim culture. *The Times*, 20 November 2015. Accessible online at http://mickhartley.typepad.com/blog/2015/11/the-false-victim-culture.html (accessed 28 January 2016).

Pope Paul VI (1965). *Nostra Aetate ('In Our Time')*. Declaration on the Relation of the Church to Non-Christian Religions. 28 October 1965. Accessible online at: www.vatican.va/archive/hist_councils/ii_vatican_council/documents/vat-ii_decl_19651028_nostra-aetate_en.html (accessed 24 January 2016).

Press Complaints Commission. *Editors' Code of Practice*. Accessible online at http://www.pcc.org.uk/assets/696/Code_of_Practice_2012_A4.pdf (accessed 29 March 2016).

Ridley, Louise (2014). Does religion cause war . . . and do atheists have something to answer for? *Huffington Post*, 14 November 2014. Accessible online at www.huffingtonpost.co.uk/2014/11/14/religions-war-cause-responsible-evidence_n_6156878.html (accessed 19 March 2016).

Rushdie, Salman (1988/1997). *The Satanic Verses*. New York: Henry Holt.

Sizer, Stephen (2013). Christian Zionism: the heresy that undermines Middle East peace. *Middle East Monitor*, 1 August 2013. Accessible online at http://www.informationclearinghouse.info/article35747.htm (accessed 3 November 2015).

Tertullian. *Apology*.

Wikipedia (2016a). *War on Terror*. Accessible online at en.wikipedia.org/wiki/War_
on_Terror (accessed 28 January 2016).

Wikipedia (2016b). *West–Eastern Divan Orchestra*. Accessible online at en.m.
wikipedia.org/wiki/West-Eastern_Divan_Orchestra (accessed 28 January 2016).

World Council of Churches (1979/2010). *Guidelines on Dialogue with People of
Living Faiths and Ideologies*. Accessible online at http://www.oikoumene.org/
en/resources/documents/wcc-programmes/interreligious-dialogue-and-
cooperation/interreligious-trust-and-respect/guidelines-on-dialogue-with-
people-of-living-faiths-and-ideologies (accessed 28 January 2016).

Index